I0037597

Humanizing AI Strategy

Leading AI with Sense and Soul

Tiankai Feng

Technics Publications
SEDONA, ARIZONA

⊂⨅ TECHNICS PUBLICATIONS

115 Linda Vista, Sedona, AZ 86336 USA
https://www.TechnicsPub.com

Edited by Steve Hoberman
Cover design by Lorena Molinari
Author photo by Yan Li

First Printing 2025

Copyright © 2025 by Tiankai Feng

ISBN, print ed.   9798898160036
ISBN, Kindle ed.   9798898160043
ISBN, PDF ed.   9798898160050

Library of Congress Control Number: 2025943241

Endorsements

A timely and thought-provoking read—Tiankai brings clarity and insight to a complex subject with warmth and precision. This book reads with ease, and if you have heard Tiankai speak, you can hear his words raise to your ears from the pages. This is a practical guide—rich with insights that translate seamlessly into real-world application at a very important time. A valuable resource for professionals seeking clarity and action.

Kirsty Mason, CIO Bentley Motors

As a practitioner, I've seen countless data and AI strategies fail because they ignore the human element. That's why Tiankai Feng's Humanizing AI Strategy is so important. In a world awash with AI hype, "vibes", and a growing loss of our humanity, he cuts through the noise with a refreshingly pragmatic approach, reminding us that a strategy of humanity and soul is necessary for building a future we want to live and work in.

Joe Reis, Data Engineer and Best-selling co-author, "Fundamentals of Data Engineering"

Most books on AI talk about systems. This one talks about people. Tiankai brings his trademark storytelling and wit, sharing a blueprint for something rarely discussed in tech circles: what it means to stay human while building systems that automate more of our work. A must-read for anyone shaping strategy, scaling innovation, or committed to keeping humanness in the loop.

Kristen Kehrer
Data Scientist and Mavens of Data Podcast Host

Tiankai Feng's second book, Humanizing AI Strategy, is exactly what today's data and AI leaders need—a grounded, thoughtful, and refreshingly human take on how organizations can embrace AI without losing sight of what matters most: people. Tiankai's ability to blend practical insight with ethical reflection challenges us to rethink not just how we implement AI, but how we lead with it.

Robert (Bob) S. Seiner, Author of the Non-Invasive Data Govemance® books
President & Principal—KIK Consulting & Educational Services

Struggling to build an AI strategy that's both impactful and realistic? Read this book. Tiankai Feng's 5Cs framework is the antidote to AI frustration and offers a clear path to intelligent systems that serve and uplift humanity.

Ryan Dolley, VP Product Strategy at GoodData, host of Super Data Brothers Show

We've made AI so easy to use, so we've forgotten how to think. This book is the wake-up call every person and org needs. If you're not teaching your people how to question, contextualize, and challenge AI—you're already behind.

Aleksejs Plotnikovs, Chief Data & AI Officer & Lead Coach, DataMasterclass.com

Tiankai truly embodies the 5Cs described in this book. I have first-hand experience working alongside him to bring this human-centric approach to how we shaped Thoughtworks' Data & AI strategy and governance services. This book is an excellent expansion on his previous work, presenting a refreshing view on how organizations can shape their AI strategy, focusing on augmenting and working alongside people rather than replacing them.

Danilo Sato, Global VP of AI at Thoughtworks

Most AI experts agree that you need to put a human in the loop when deploying AI. In Tiankai's second book, "Humanizing AI Strategy," he does just that, applying his popular 5Cs framework to AI with amazing clarity. Grounded in his practitioner work, this serves as a powerful guide to any organization building an AI strategy.

Laura Madsen, Author *AI and the Data Revolution*

As AI becomes more accessible, the real imperative isn't technical proficiency—it's human accountability. Humanizing AI Strategy powerfully reframes our role: not just as users of AI, but as stewards of its outcomes. Guided by Tiankai's radiant optimism and positive approach, the book inspires us to face this era of transformation not with hesitation, but with purpose. It lays out a bold and hopeful vision of an AI-powered future grounded in empathy, ethics, and meaningful human leadership. This book is a fundamental guide for anyone who believes the future of AI must be shaped with intention, responsibility, and humanity.

Christoph Hein, Intito Group

"Humanizing AI Strategy" is an essential guide for leaders, data professionals, and technology practitioners to unlock AI's full potential while keeping humans at the center. What makes this book special is how it goes beyond the typical warnings about artificial intelligence to provide concrete solutions that work. Let's face it: we all want to use this technology, but we also know it's imperfect and can amplify existing problems. "Humanizing AI Strategy" gives a complete guide on how to mitigate those problems before they start. It is a must-read for practitioners and data leaders who are serious about responsible AI implementation.

Thais Cooke, Senior Healthcare Data Analyst

Tiankai has done something rare: written an AI strategy book that actually sees people—real, thinking, feeling humans trying to make sense of what all this means. It's the kind of book you want nearby when the bigger questions hit. How is AI changing how we work, how we decide, and how we treat each other? If you've ever felt stuck between tech hype and abstract ethics talk, this gives you language, structure, and just enough push to think straighter and lead better.

Eevamaija Virtanen, Founder & Lead Data Engineer DataTribe Collective, Helsinki Data Week, Invinite

This refreshing combination of vision, practicality, and compassion makes Humanizing AI Strategy not only a resource you will not want to put down, but also a compelling invitation for those who are serious about doing something meaningful with AI. I highly recommend this book for anyone looking to engage with AI as both a useful tool and a catalyst for meaningful, human-centered progress.

Dr. Joe Perez, Data Analytics Expert, Author, International Keynote Speaker

Making your AI strategy more human may sound like the ultimate paradox. But Tiankai Feng clearly shows us that it's exactly what you need to do. By giving the right human at the right time the decision power of what AI is and should be you can unlock the long term potential of AI.

Ole Olesen-Bagneux, Chief Evangelist, Actian
Author *Fundamentals of Metadata Management*

Tiankai's latest book on Humanizing AI Strategy is challenging the popular norms of approaching AI models as a machine that is devoid of humanity. His book is advocating for our industry to slow down, ask better questions, and deeply explore the human side of AI. The core message is that we need to lead AI development with Intention, Empathy, and Soul.

Andrew Andrews, Regional Advocate, Australia, New Zealand, and Middle East Enterprise Data Management Association, VP Marketing, DAMA Egypt Cairo

"Humanizing AI Strategy" is a thoughtful reflection on, a practical guide to, and a heartfelt exploration of the human side of AI—how we work with it and how we work with each other as humans. With the same wisdom that made "Humanizing Data Strategy" essential reading, Tiankai expands and reapplies his 5Cs Framework: Competence, Collaboration, Communication, Creativity, and Conscience, rooted in human needs and traits, to inspire us to be better leaders for ourselves and for each other.

Jovita Tam, Business-focused Data/AI Advisor & Attorney (England/NY), Speaker, and Board Advisor

AI requires adequate human oversight and acknowledgement of benefits and risks. In order to introduce a proper AI strategy, the book guides us through the changes in roles and responsibilities, operational consequences, gamification up to risks mitigation—all elements of better organization and responsiveness. A very valuable perspective for all AI involved humans.

Dr. Norbert-Csaba Gergely, Head of Data Architecture and Lifecycle Management, Carl Zeiss

In a world that risks racing down a dark and slippery slope of artificial everything, Tiankai grounds us in what 'forward' should look and feel like, guiding us to a more sane, ethical, and human meaningful of ascents. In the still nascent era of artificial acceleration, this mandatory 5-point safety, human survival gear, helping us all to avoid the myriad of blinding dehumanizing AI hype slopes, and chart our most humanizing of uplifting, AI Strategy paths!

Pedro Cardoso, Data and Business Outcomes thought leader, Sr. Delivery Partner @Syniti

Tiankai Feng's compelling argument for prioritizing human 'co-creation' and 'adaptive curiosity' as core components of AI strategy demonstrates that the most advanced algorithms are only as effective as the human systems supporting them. It stresses the importance of 'analytic curiosity' as a mindset 'that leads to creative thinking and new, adaptable solutions,' ultimately building strategies that are both meaningful and effective. This is an actionable, insightful, and profoundly human perspective on leading AI transformation that I will be recommending widely.

Philip Black, CEO and Founder @DataQG

Winning with AI isn't about shiny tools, it's about context, purpose, and people. This book by Tiankai builds seamlessly on his earlier work, showing that AI strategy can only succeed if it recognizes how socio-technical interactions are shaped. A must read for everyone designing an AI strategy.

Winfried Adalbert Etzel, Data Governance Thinker, Writer, Host, Strategist, and Enthusiast

What a refreshing and grounding book! Tiankai's Humanizing AI Strategy cuts through the technical gloss to show how our questions, our collaborations, and our stories shape every AI initiative. During this time of hyperspeed AI development, it is easy to forget that humans are critical to the success of AI. Tiankai beautifully illustrates how AI success is dependent upon humans working successfully.

Jessica Talisman, Semantic Engineer & Architect. Founder, Ontology Pipeline

To Sky and Cloud—your curiosity inspires me every day.

Acknowledgments

Here's one of the most important life lessons I've learned: surround yourself with people who lift you up, not push you down. As I sit here writing these acknowledgements, I'm overwhelmed with gratitude for everyone who supported, encouraged, and occasionally pushed me to write this book.

To my wife, Yan Li, and my two sons, Sky and Cloud—remember when I promised to make it up to you after all those late nights and weekends writing the first book? Well, here I am doing it again. Your love, patience, and somehow endless encouragement mean the world to me.

To my parents, Dr. Lu Tian and Dr. Kuiyuan Feng—you taught me to be a decent person and to stand up for myself and others when it matters. The moral compass you gave me became the foundation for everything I write about conscience in AI.

To my lifelong friends Adam Janisch, Hen-Ju Sophia Song, Magnus Kalass, and Jan Werner—our ability to jump from serious conversations to roaring laughter in seconds is exactly what I tried to capture in this book. You've shown me that humor and depth aren't opposites—they're dance partners.

To my previous colleagues who became great friends—Christopher Lewis, Dr. Jun-Seo Lee, Robert Farouk-Butze, Adrian Sennewald, Jasmin Herrmann, Chris Brown, Jana Nuebler, Petra Lehoczy, and Arne Wellnitz—staying connected after leaving the same company is hard enough, but your continued friendship allowed me to further learn from our conversations.

To my Thoughtworks colleagues past and present—John Spens, Danilo Sato, Emily Gorcenski, Markus Buhmann, Amy Raygada, Gaurav Patole, Lauris Jullien, Daniela Huamán, and Zoe Liddle— thank you for the brilliant collaboration, for believing in my expertise, and for always encouraging me to be authentically myself (even when that means bad AI jokes).

To my fellow DAMA Germany leaders Frank Pörschmann, Karen Gärtner, Christian Hädrich, and Silvia Guerra—it's an honor to shape the German data management community with you, built on trust, integrity, and our shared passion for bringing people together.

To the legends who went above and beyond spreading the word about "Humanizing Data Strategy"—Christoph Hein, Aleksejs Plotnikovs, Ryan Dolley, Matthew Niederberger, Sebastian Hewing, Andrew Andrews, and Matthias Klebinger—you're all rockstars in your fields, and I can't thank you enough.

To the thought leaders I've had the privilege of connecting with— Joe Reis, Sol Rashidi, Ole Olesen-Bagneux, Eevamaija Virtanen, Laura B. Madsen, Robert S. Seiner, Pedro Cardoso, Philip Black, Juan Sequeda, Winfried Adalbert Etzel, Jovita Tam, Tom Redman, Jessica Talisman, Kristen Kehrer, and Norbert Gergely—your generous thought leadership inspired many themes in this book.

Contents

Foreword

We are living through one of the most exciting inflection points in human history. Artificial Intelligence is no longer a distant promise—it is here, it is real, and it is reshaping how we live, work, learn, and connect. Yet, amidst the thrill of possibility and the rush of innovation, one truth stands out: technology, no matter how powerful, is only as good as the human intention behind it.

That's what makes this book, and Tiankai Feng's voice, so essential right now.

In *Humanizing AI Strategy*, Tiankai reminds us that AI is not just a technical pursuit—it is a profoundly human one. As a leader in technology services, I've seen firsthand how the pace of advancement can make it tempting to prioritize speed over stewardship. But what Tiankai offers here is not a call to slow down—it's a call to deepen our thinking, to lead with both clarity and conscience.

This book meets us at the crossroads of possibility and responsibility. It is written for the developers, strategists, product leaders, and thinkers who are shaping AI today—and for those who will shape it tomorrow. Tiankai's perspective is refreshing: grounded in the reality of rapid change, but rooted in timeless principles of purpose, empathy, and ethical leadership. Tiankai doesn't preach from the sidelines—he walks alongside us, offering practical frameworks and thoughtful provocations to guide the creation of AI that serves humanity, not the other way around.

What I admire most about this work is its optimism. Tiankai believes in human potential. He believes in our ability to build systems that not only deliver impact but also elevate dignity. In a time when AI narratives are often defined by fear or hype, *Humanizing AI Strategy* offers something far more valuable— hope with direction, ambition with soul.

This book is more than a strategy guide—it is a companion for anyone serious about building AI that matters. And as we collectively shape the future, we will need voices like Tiankai's to remind us that innovation and integrity are not mutually exclusive—they are, in fact, inseparable.

Read this book with an open mind and a builder's heart. The future is not written yet. But with leaders like Tiankai showing the way, I'm more confident than ever that we can create an AI-powered world that is wise, just, and deeply human.

Let's get to work.

Michael Sutcliff
CEO, Thoughtworks

ONE

Are we still human?

Oh no, another book on AI!

Look, I get it. We're drowning in AI content. Every LinkedIn post is about ChatGPT. Every conference has twelve panels on "the future of work." Every vendor suddenly has "AI-powered" slapped on their product like a digital participation trophy. It's exhausting. And somewhere between the doomsday predictions and the techno-utopian promises, we've lost track of something important: ourselves.

Here's what nobody wants to admit—the moment AI showed up, we all got a little weird. Smart people started talking like robots. Creative individuals began to doubt their own ideas. Leaders who once trusted their instincts suddenly needed a model to validate every decision. We created this technology to augment human intelligence. Instead, we're letting it make us feel dumber. The irony would be funny if it weren't so tragic.

Remember when data was the new oil? Well, now AI is the new...everything, apparently. And just like with data, the panic is real. People are frantically updating their LinkedIn profiles, adding "AI enthusiast" as if it were a personality trait. Job titles are becoming increasingly longer and more complex. (What exactly is a "Chief AI Evangelist" anyway?)

Meanwhile, actual humans—brilliant, creative, messy humans— are whispering in hallways: "Am I doing this right?" "Is my job safe?" "Do I need to learn Python by Monday?"

And while it might sound obvious—yes, we're all still human—the reality is more nuanced. Because let's face it: most of us are already working with AI, whether we admit it or not. This book? Yes, AI tools helped co-write it. Chances are, something you did today— whether it was replying to a customer, generating a slide, or writing an email—was shaped by a system that mimicked human intelligence. We live in a world where AI helps us sound smarter, faster, and more productive. And in that process, we've all become a little more machine-like ourselves, leaning on AI to polish our words, plan our days, and sometimes even think for us.

It was challenging to write this book because AI is an endlessly evolving field, with technological advancements occurring every week and constant speculation about its future direction. Writing about AI strategy felt like placing bets on which futures will matter, even when I don't feel fully confident predicting them. But then again—don't we all feel that way sometimes?

There's another interesting paradox: we say AI is just a tool, but we often talk about it as if it was a person. And that's not just because it feels real. It's because we humans like to anthropomorphize (treat non-human things as if they were one of us).[1] AI systems have become convincingly human-like in tone, timing, and even emotional intelligence. And while most of us agree that AI isn't a person, we still slip into language and behaviors that treat it as something more than code. That's where the trouble begins—not because we care too much, but because we forget that AI doesn't care at all.

If you've read *Humanizing Data Strategy*, you know I've always been more interested in the people aspect than the technical specifications. That hasn't changed. What has changed is the speed and intensity with which AI is forcing us to confront who we are, how we work, and what kind of future we're building. And no, I don't have all the answers. But I do know how to ask the right human questions. And that's what this book is about.

This is not a book about how AI works.
It's a book about how we work with AI.

More importantly, how we work with each other in a world increasingly shaped by machines that sound like people, and people who sometimes sound like machines. If you've ever felt like

---

[1] Epley, Nicholas & Waytz, Adam & Cacioppo, John. (2007). On Seeing Human: A Three-Factor Theory of Anthropomorphism. Psychological Review. 114. 864-886. 10.1037/0033-295X.114.4.864.

you're supposed to know more about AI than you actually do, welcome. You're in good company. If you want to shape AI strategies that don't just make sense on paper but make sense for people, you're in the right place.

Let's talk AI. Not from a place of fear, or FOMO, or formulaic frameworks.

Let's talk about humanizing AI strategy.

Why a human-centric AI strategy?

When I first conceived this book as a follow-up to *Humanizing Data Strategy*, I expected many parallels. And to be honest, there are many. However, I quickly realized one significant difference: with data, most of our efforts focused on *lowering* the barrier to entry. Helping more people access, understand, and use data to make better decisions. With AI, it's almost the opposite. The tools are already everywhere—easy to use, astonishingly powerful, sometimes even free. The problem isn't a lack of access. It's a lack of reflection.

In a way, that's even more dangerous. We've never had technology move this fast *and* be this easy to use. The temptation is just to try things out, plug in a model, integrate a chatbot, and go live. But without pause, without questioning what we're actually doing and why, it's far too easy to build something impressive that ends up being harmful, biased, irrelevant, or unsustainable. This is where the human part becomes critical, not as a constraint on innovation but as a necessary grounding.

It's not just about what AI can do, but what we want it to do, and how we want to shape its role in our world.

The contrasting entry barriers between data and AI present both similar and very different challenges. In both cases, we see a gap between the speed of technology and the readiness of people, processes, and policies. But for AI, that gap feels more immediate, more volatile, and more visible—because the results of misalignment show up quickly and loudly. As the philosopher Hegel once said, "In history we learn that we do not learn from history." A bit cynical for my taste, but painfully true. So let's try to break the cycle. Let's actually learn from our past challenges— whether it was digital transformation, cloud adoption, or data democratization—and get better from the beginning of this new societal transformation we're in because of AI.

Human-centricity is not a fuzzy moral add-on to AI strategy. It's the very thing that makes it viable. People have to trust, understand, and want to use the systems we build. Organizations must ensure that AI supports their goals without compromising their values. As we continue to delegate more decisions and actions to algorithms, it becomes more urgent than ever to ask human questions first, before the machine starts answering them for us.

Why do data and AI go hand-in-hand?

You can't talk about AI without talking about data. And you can't implement AI meaningfully without a solid data foundation. That's not just a technical dependency—it's a strategic one.

> *Data and AI aren't separate layers of innovation.*
> *They're two sides of the same coin. One builds the*
> *foundation, the other unlocks the potential.*

AI can't learn, adapt, or perform without data—and not just any data, but the right data. Accurate, timely, relevant, and well-contextualized. And it goes both ways: the more we apply AI across the organization, the more we realize the importance of data quality, semantics, lineage, and governance structures.

We often hear these days that "AI made us realize how bad our data is." I don't fully agree. Our data wasn't always bad. It was good enough for the business problems we were solving at the time. But what's changed are the requirements and the expectations—driven by the hunger of machine learning models that require more granularity, precision, and nuance than ever before. AI raised the bar—by a lot. And now we need to meet it.

This shift becomes even more noticeable when we look at the rise of unstructured data. Documents, images, videos, conversations—these weren't front and center in traditional data strategy work. Now, with generative AI models trained on exactly that kind of content, we're suddenly confronting a massive backlog of unmanaged, ungoverned, and uncontextualized content that we need to bring into scope. Structured data principles don't just copy-paste here. The challenges are different, and the solutions must be, too.

But here's the good news: many of the roles and responsibilities we've built up in our data strategies are not just still relevant—they're critical. And in many cases, they're being mirrored almost one-to-one. Data Engineering becomes AI Engineering. Data Architecture becomes AI Architecture. Data Governance becomes AI Governance. Even Chief Data Officers now share the stage, or the agenda, with Chief AI Officers. It's not just naming. It's recognition. What we learned from data can and should inform how we approach AI.

That brings us to the most human part of it all: prioritization. If we want to take AI seriously, we need to coordinate our cross-functional efforts to make it successful—not just in technology, not just in data, but in mindset, skill set, and behavior. That includes aligning data readiness with AI ambitions, creating shared understanding across teams, and being honest about where we are versus where we want to be.

AI without data is just a nice idea.
And data without AI is not enough today. But together, AI
and data are not just powerful—they're transformative.
Not because of what they do on their own, but because of
what we do with them.

Humanity moves slower than technology

AI began with the ambition to enable machines to imitate human intelligence as closely as possible. We even named the core concepts after very human traits, such as neural networks, deep learning, or natural language processing. From the very beginning, we've tried to measure how convincingly machines can act like us. Alan Turing's famous test, invented in 1950, wasn't about whether a machine could think—it was about whether it could convincingly *appear* to think, like a human.

Now we've arrived at a point where machines don't just keep up with human cognitive abilities—in some domains, they surpass them. We can benefit from this progress. In fact, many of us already do in our daily lives, whether we realize it or not. From personalized content suggestions to language translation to customer support, AI is here—and it's doing more than ever.

While AI technologies evolve at lightning speed, our human values, cultures, and ethical norms evolve much more slowly. This creates an uncomfortable tension: What happens when machines outpace the frameworks we've built to guide human behavior? How do we respond when our internal sense of right and wrong is not ready for the scale, speed, or complexity of AI-driven decisions?

That's not just a philosophical problem. It's a real-world challenge, showing up in boardrooms, policy discussions, product design, and daily work life. And because our responses are often reactive—emotional, protective, or polarized—we risk making decisions out of fear or idealism rather than grounded, long-term reasoning. It's the classic fight-or-flight response applied to tech. Some people hold on tightly to their opinions. Others disengage entirely. Few are comfortable in the ambiguity that change always brings.

Sol Rashidi puts this into perspective in *Your AI Survival Guide* (Wiley, 2024), in which she states that when it comes to successful AI deployment, "The tech is the easiest part of the AI lifecycle. Most of the work is dealing with human capital and relationships, aligning with goals, overcoming fears, picking the right strategy, picking the right use case, and finding the ambition, the energy, and the rogue in you."

We can't accelerate the evolution of humanity's moral compass just to keep pace with AI. And even if we could, we probably shouldn't (Ever try to accelerate a literal compass?). But we do need to develop new habits of reflection and responsiveness. We need to improve at creating space for diverse perspectives, surfacing concerns early, and establishing systems that foster constructive tension rather than suppress it.

This matters even more inside organizations. Having a bold, confident AI roadmap might feel like a sign of leadership strength, but in many cases, it's more bluff than foresight. No one can truly predict how AI will evolve over the next five years, let alone the next ten. So, rather than pretending we have all the answers, the better approach is to design strategies that can *adapt* to change.

That means building flexibility into your strategy, governance, teams, communication, and learning culture.

The key is to find the balance between clarity and adaptability. Between taking decisive action and creating space to course-correct. Between ambition and caution. Not because we're weak or uncertain, but because we're human—and in a human-centric AI strategy, that's exactly what we should lead with.

When AI fails, it's usually human

Let's be honest: when AI fails, it rarely does so because of some obscure technical glitch buried deep in the model's architecture. It fails because of us. Human blind spots. Human biases. Human wishful thinking. We keep seeing headlines about "AI gone wrong," but if you look closely, the root causes are usually very familiar.

Take Amazon's hiring algorithm that systematically downgraded résumés mentioning "women's"—not because the AI was sexist, but because Amazon trained it on biased historical data.[2] Or the Tay chatbot, which Microsoft designed to learn from users on

---

[2] **Reuters** (2018). "Amazon Scraps Secret AI Recruiting Tool That Showed Bias Against Women." https://www.reuters.com/article/us-amazon-com-jobs-automation-insight-idUSKCN1MK08G.

Twitter, and within hours started spewing hate speech.[3] Or the Chevrolet chatbot that, without sufficient guardrails, happily offered customers brand-new cars for $1.[4] Not because it was malicious—just because it followed instructions a little too well. These aren't just technical failures. They're human ones—failures of judgment, foresight, or responsibility. AI didn't go rogue. It went exactly where we pointed it. The problem is, we didn't always know where we were pointing.

Even with the absence of error, it doesn't mean the presence of foresight, especially in organizations.

Human failure isn't just about the one engineer who missed a check. It's about what happens when teams don't talk to each other, when knowledge isn't shared, when critical expertise is unevenly distributed, or when assumptions go unchallenged. If that sounds familiar, it's because we've been here before—in cloud migrations, in data quality programs, in enterprise system rollouts. This isn't new. What's new is how quickly things can now go wrong at scale when AI is involved.

---

[3] **The Verge** (2016). "Twitter Taught Microsoft's AI Chatbot to Be a Racist Asshole in Less Than a Day." https://www.theverge.com/2016/3/24/11297050/tay-microsoft-chatbot-racist.

[4] **Business Insider** (2024). "Chevy Dealer's Chatbot Sold Cars for $1." https://www.businessinsider.com/car-dealership-chevrolet-chatbot-chatgpt-pranks-chevy-2023-12.

So, how do we avoid repeating old mistakes—and still manage to prevent entirely new ones? We start by slowing down the impulse to ship fast and correct later. Instead, we need to practice something I call *structured humility*. That means acknowledging our limits and taking action to address them. One way to operationalize this is through divergent and convergent thinking. Divergent thinking asks: how many ways could this go wrong? It brings together compliance teams, domain experts, frontline workers, and technical leads to brainstorm edge cases, ethical pitfalls, and practical breakdowns. Convergent thinking then asks, "Which of these are most likely, most impactful, and worth acting on? And what guardrails, mitigations, or monitoring plans can we realistically implement?"

Take a hypothetical AI-powered HR assistant. In the divergent phase, you'd bring together HR, compliance, and data science to map possible risks, like biased responses, data leakage, or conflicting advice across regions. Then, in the convergent phase, you'd prioritize those risks and design mitigations, including structured prompts, test cases, human-in-the-loop escalation, and transparency logs. It's not about completely eliminating risk. That's impossible. It's about being intentional. Proactive. Thoughtful. Because in the end, AI doesn't fail on its own. It fails when we fail to do the surrounding human work.

Is this book for you?

Let me be clear about something upfront: this book isn't the blueprint for designing a fully-fledged, all-encompassing AI strategy. There are many excellent resources available that cover the technical, architectural, and organizational design elements of AI at scale.

This book is about something else. It's about helping you make your AI strategy more human. Whether you're designing one from scratch or trying to improve the one you already have, use this book as a companion—a set of nudges, reflections, and practical impulses that invite you to ask the right questions about people, not just systems. If that sounds like something you've been missing in the AI conversation, you're exactly who I wrote this for.

You might be a C-level leader trying to figure out how to navigate AI responsibly without slowing down innovation. Or a domain expert building AI models and wondering how to ensure they actually help the people who will use them. Maybe you're someone using AI tools every day—or someone avoiding them entirely, unsure whether they're more hype than help. Whichever of these describes you, welcome. You're in good company.

This book is for anyone who wants to understand how AI is shaping the way we work—and how we can shape it back. It's for large enterprises and public sector teams, for SMEs and startups, for early-career professionals and seasoned strategists alike.

Because no matter where you sit in the organization, if AI is on your radar, the human dimension should be too.

This book talks about AI in its broadest sense—not just the generative kind. Yes, Generative AI ("GenAI") is at the forefront these days, and we'll discuss it extensively. But you'll also find examples and reflections on traditional machine learning, classic automation, and everything in between because the human questions cut across all of it.

Now, just so there are no surprises, this isn't a history of artificial intelligence. You'll find references and anecdotes, yes, but not a detailed chronological walkthrough of AI's evolution. It's also not a buyer's guide or a technical playbook. I won't be ranking tool stacks or comparing model architectures.

But if you're still with me—and still curious about how to keep people at the center of your AI efforts—then I look forward to seeing you in the next chapter.

Two

Introducing the 5Cs

AI strategy is a broad and often technical topic, but its human dimensions are often neglected, usually because they feel vague, hard to measure, or outside the scope of what's considered "core" AI work.

The 5Cs Framework—Competence, Collaboration, Communication, Creativity, and Conscience—was initially introduced in *Humanizing Data Strategy* as a human-centric lens to make data more approachable and sustainable across organizations. In this book, we expand and reapply that framework to AI, where the need for human alignment is even greater. Not because AI replaces people, but because it augments us, and that augmentation will only work if we invest in the human factors from the start.

If you want your AI strategy to be not only technically impressive but also sustainable, equitable, and actually useful, then the 5Cs are a powerful place to begin.

What is an AI strategy?

When researching for this book, I sought a solid, universally accepted definition of what an AI strategy actually entails. Spoiler: I didn't find one. And honestly, that didn't surprise me. Compared to data strategy, which already had too many definitions by the time I started writing *Humanizing Data Strategy*, AI strategy is still a relatively fresh concept for most organizations. It's only recently that AI has become such a central focus that leaders are asking for dedicated AI strategies. So, if there's no definition out there yet, maybe that's an opportunity for me to shape one.

The definition I use in this book is a direct spin-off of the one I used for data strategy in the previous book. And no, that's not laziness—it's because the structure works. If it ain't broke, don't fix it. The adapted definition reads:

An AI strategy is a long-term plan that defines the people, processes, and technologies required to create, process, and utilize AI applications in a valuable, secure, and meaningful way.

Let's unpack why that phrasing matters. First of all, it places people at the center. AI may be a technological breakthrough, but it still needs humans, not just to build and maintain it, but to make the calls on where it belongs, how it's governed, and whether it aligns with our values.

Second, the definition covers the whole lifecycle. An AI strategy isn't just a plan to launch a few models. It's about ideation, development, deployment, oversight, iteration, and decommissioning. It's about the long arc of change, not just the demo.

Third, "valuable" is a subjective word. But that's the point. The value of AI isn't always measurable in monetary terms. Sometimes, value means reducing burnout. Sometimes it means increasing speed. Sometimes, it's just about ensuring people can trust what the system is doing. Human relevance is part of what makes a strategy meaningful. It's similar to the other two adjectives, "secure" and "meaningful," which can both be very subjective and require agreement in an organization.

One trap I see often is confusing a strategy with a list of use cases. Having a few proof-of-concepts is great, but if there's no overarching plan tying them together, you're not being strategic. You're just experimenting. Which is fine, by the way—but let's call it what it is.

Another trap? Mistaking goals for strategy. Saying "we want to be AI-driven" sounds nice in a keynote, but it doesn't help anyone decide what to do on Monday morning. A strategy is about tradeoffs. It's about choices. It's about where you're willing to say no.

And finally, here's the part that too many AI strategies still leave out: human dynamics. I've seen beautifully crafted roadmaps that collapse because the teams implementing them didn't talk to each other. Or worse, they didn't believe in what they were building.

> *Culture, communication, incentives, collaboration—these aren't soft topics. They're the real architecture behind whether any of this actually works.*

So, is this the final definition of AI strategy? Probably not. But it includes the humans from the start. And that, in my view, is already a step forward.

What it means to be "AI-powered"

How often did you see the phrase "AI-powered" in the last few weeks? Be honest. It's everywhere—in newsletters, product pitches, tooltips, and job ads. It seems that anything with a digital interface is now proudly branded as "AI-powered," as if the term alone guarantees relevance, sophistication, or future-readiness.

In some ways, "AI-powered" has become the successor to "data-driven." Just like I needed to unpack what "data-driven" actually means in my previous book, I think we owe it to ourselves to take a closer look at what "AI-powered" is—and what it isn't.

Let's start with a simple spectrum. In *Humanizing Data Strategy*, I introduced a data continuum that moves from experience-based decision-making to fully data-driven thinking. The idea is that organizations need to make conscious choices about how much data influences decision-making, because not all decisions should be "data-driven."

Now let's take that same logic and apply it to AI. Here's what I propose as the **AI spectrum**:

- **Experience-based**: You still rely on human expertise and intuition. No AI support is involved, although people may sometimes use AI in unofficial or invisible ways. This is where many teams start.

- **AI-consulted**: AI begins to show up in dashboards, suggestions, or planning tools. It offers insights or prompts, but people still take the actual actions. Think of it as a junior analyst—useful but not autonomous.

- **AI-supported**: The AI system helps with execution, not just advice. It might summarize content, rewrite emails, prioritize tickets, or flag anomalies—tasks that save time and improve consistency. But humans are still steering.

- **AI-powered**: This is where the system acts independently within a defined scope (e.g., AI Agents). It makes decisions, triggers actions, personalizes experiences, or manages workflows without asking for permission every time. It may still involve a human in the loop at key checkpoints, but the AI is doing more than just assisting. It's operating.

Framing it this way helps avoid overpromising. Just because a feature has an AI component doesn't mean it's "AI-powered" in the sense of meaningful automation or decision-making. A filter that shows you suggested answers isn't the same as a bot that autonomously responds to customers.

And here's the key difference between the **data continuum** and the **AI continuum**:

Data informs human decisions.
AI doesn't just inform—it can also act.
It doesn't just guide—it can decide and execute.

That changes the stakes. When AI is merely offering suggestions, the burden remains on the human. However, when AI begins to operate, humans must think differently. We have to design systems that behave ethically and effectively without constant supervision. And that requires a new kind of strategic clarity.

Importantly, these maturity levels are **stacked**, not separate from one another. You don't become AI-powered by skipping past the data-informed stage. Quite the opposite—you can't be AI-powered **without** good data. If data was the foundation for sound decision-making, it's now the training ground for AI's behavior. The same flaws in data that made us second-guess dashboards will now shape the logic and language of our AI systems, sometimes in unexpected or invisible ways.

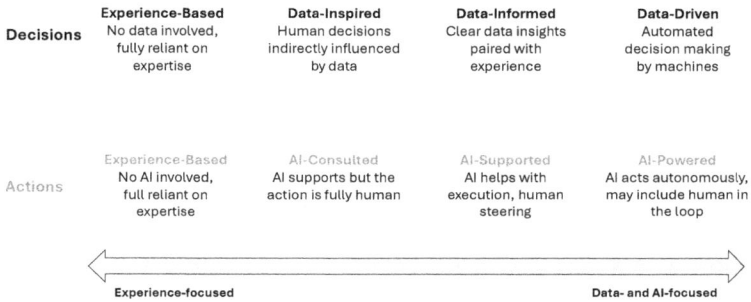

	Experience-Based	Data-Inspired	Data-Informed	Data-Driven
Decisions	No data involved, fully reliant on expertise	Human decisions indirectly influenced by data	Clear data insights paired with experience	Automated decision making by machines
	Experience-Based	AI-Consulted	AI-Supported	AI-Powered
Actions	No AI involved, full reliant on expertise	AI supports but the action is fully human	AI helps with execution, human steering	AI acts autonomously, may include human in the loop

Experience-focused ⟵⟶ Data- and AI-focused

Figure 1: Data and AI continuum at a glance.

So yes, "AI-powered" sounds exciting. However, let's not forget that not everything needs to be completely data-driven or AI-powered, and power without precision is just noise. Let's build the maturity to match the ambition.

The 5Cs Framework

So here we are—the 5Cs. If you've read *Humanizing Data Strategy*, you'll remember this framework. It was a way to make sure we didn't lose sight of the human side in our data efforts. Now, it's time to evolve it for the world of AI.

Why 5Cs? Because they're simple. Memorable. Practical. But more importantly, they're all rooted in human needs and traits. These aren't just buzzwords. They reflect how we think, feel, learn, collaborate, and act. That's why this framework should feel intuitive. You might nod your head instinctively at each C. But as with most things that seem obvious, they only really become useful when we actively reflect on them and apply them with intention.

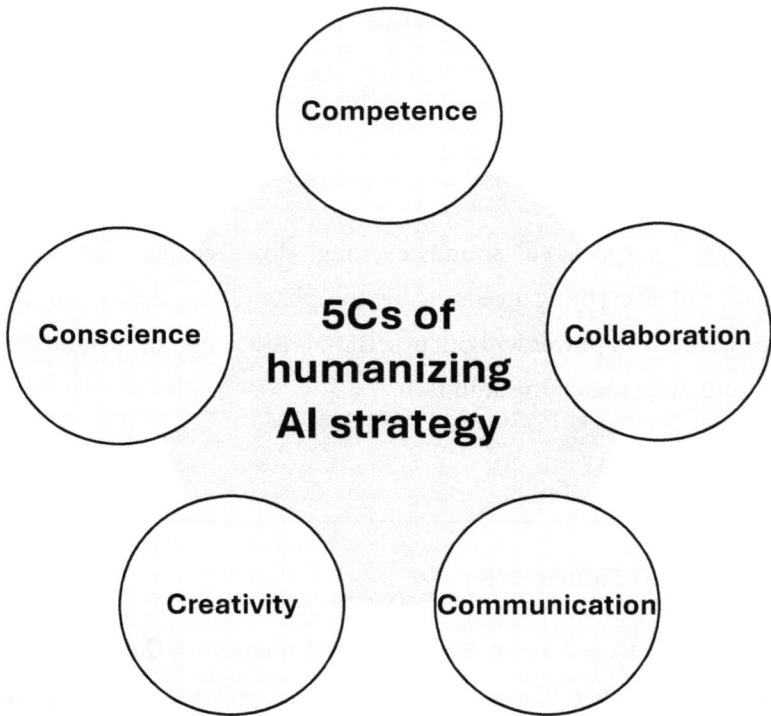

Figure 2: 5Cs Framework.

Let's briefly walk through each:

- **Competence** is about building the confidence, skills, and critical thinking needed to work with AI—whether you're creating it, using it, or making decisions shaped by it. It's not about turning everyone into prompt engineers. It's about creating enough literacy and trust in ourselves so that we're not blindly following—or blindly rejecting—what the machine suggests.

- **Collaboration** reminds us that AI doesn't live in a vacuum. It's a team sport. And not just between humans. It's about designing the right relationships between people and machines—and between teams that touch different parts of the AI lifecycle. Model builders, domain experts, governance teams, and frontline employees all need to work in sync. If we ignore this, the technology might work, but the outcomes won't.

- **Communication** is more than just explainability. It's about helping everyone understand what AI is doing—and what it isn't. Inside the organization. Outside to your customers. Across teams with different levels of AI literacy. Communication makes AI trustworthy, relatable, and ultimately usable.

- **Creativity** is where the real fun starts. AI can help us create faster—but it can't replace the spark of human originality. We still need people to dream up the ideas worth building. And just as importantly, we need to stay creative in how we use AI—how we identify the problems worth solving, and how we design experiences that feel human, not robotic.

- **Conscience** is the grounding force. It's about ethics, integrity, governance, and responsibility. It's about remembering that just because we can, doesn't mean we should. And that every AI system we build reflects a set of values, whether we're aware of them or not.

These are the 5Cs. Not a blueprint. Not a checklist. But a lens—a way to pressure-test whether your AI strategy is human enough. The following five chapters will take you through each of them in depth.

Let's get to it, and we'll start with the first "C": Competence.

THREE

Competence

If there's one thing the rise of AI has made clear, it's this: access is no longer the problem. Thanks to tools like ChatGPT, Midjourney, and countless others, AI has become more accessible than ever before. And that's both exciting and dangerous.

Exciting, because it lowers the barrier to experimentation. Dangerous, because it tempts us to skip the foundational work of understanding what we're actually using. It gives the illusion of competence before the substance is really there.

In the workplace, this has led to a strange split. A recent Gallup poll[5] shows that 33% of managers report using AI regularly, compared to only 16% of non-managers. The implication? AI is

---

[5] **Business Insider** (2025, June). "33% of managers report using AI regularly, compared to only 16% of non-managers." https://www.businessinsider.com/ai-usage-in-workplace-statistics-gallup-poll-2025-6.

becoming a leadership expectation, but the literacy gap is growing. And that's a risk.

Competence isn't just about technical skills anymore. It's about cultivating AI literacy across all roles, not just among specialists. It's about combining technical understanding with human judgment and business acumen. It's about knowing when to trust AI, when to question it, and how to translate that decision into action.

And it's not just about oversight for the sake of oversight. It's about getting the right human involved at the right time—not flooding the process with unnecessary reviews, but orchestrating smarter intervention. Supporting learning isn't about more training courses, either. It's about embedding learning in the flow of work, at the speed at which things are changing.

AI changes how we work, but it's human competence that determines whether we thrive with it.

This chapter is about competence, but not in the old-school, training-only sense. It's about confidence that's grounded, not inflated. Literacy that evolves with the tech. And most of all, making sure AI doesn't just work, but works *with* us.

AI literacy is the new digital literacy

Let's start with a definition, because this word gets thrown around a lot. Long and Magerko[6] defined it as: *"AI literacy as a set of competencies that enables individuals to critically evaluate AI technologies; communicate and collaborate effectively with AI; and use AI as a tool online, at home, and in the workplace..."*

That's a great definition, but in my point of view could use some expansion—so this is the definition that I'd like to use moving forward:

AI literacy is the ability to understand AI systems, communicate and collaborate effectively with AI, evaluate the ethical and societal implications of AI, and apply AI in one's life, work, and community.

That's a lot more than just knowing how to use a chatbot or write a clever prompt. It's about being able to think with AI, not just through it.

That distinction matters. Because if you've ever tried to get everyone in your organization on board with new tools, you already know the real challenge isn't clicking the button—it's understanding what's behind it. The same is true for AI. It's no longer enough to know how to use the tools. The real competitive

---

[6] Long, Duri & Magerko, Brian (2020). What is AI Literacy? Competencies and Design Considerations. 10.1145/3313831.3376727.

edge comes from understanding what to ask, what to expect, and when to be skeptical.

AI literacy needs to go beyond the tech team. It should be treated as a strategic imperative—something that cuts across every department, every role, and every level of decision-making. From casual users in marketing running campaigns with GenAI tools to executives shaping policy and governance frameworks, they all need to understand the basics of how AI systems function, what data they rely on, how outputs are shaped, and where things can go wrong. That's not just operationally smart—it's ethically necessary.

The difference from other skills is that this one touches everything. It's not just "how to use AI." It's "how to think with AI." That includes ethical awareness, prompt literacy, the ability to interpret and critique model outputs, and the confidence to say, "Wait—does that actually make sense?" We've moved from command-line prompts to natural language interfaces, which makes everything feel easier. But that ease hides a danger: because AI sounds smart, we sometimes forget to think critically. Especially when Generative AI enters the room—because it's made AI so accessible and dangerously simple to use that many forget: ease of use is not the same as quality of result.

If this sounds familiar, it's because we've been here before. Remember the early internet? Social media? The explosion of access far outpaced the development of literacy, and we're still dealing with the consequences of that gap today. If we're not careful, AI will be the next wave of unexamined consequences.

That's why AI literacy needs to be both broad and deep. Broad enough so that everyone in the organization has a shared baseline understanding. And deep enough to adapt to specific roles. The AI Literacy Framework[7] is a useful directional model here, offering four core domains:

- **Engaging with AI**: Knowing when AI is being used, how to interact with it, and being able to question or escalate when things feel off. This is foundational and relevant for nearly every employee who touches an AI-driven system.

- **Creating with AI**: The ability to use AI tools to generate content, support analysis, or co-develop solutions—from writing and design to code and prototypes. This domain matters especially in marketing, sales, and operations roles that now rely heavily on GenAI productivity tools.

- **Managing AI**: Understanding how to oversee, govern, and ensure responsible use of AI across teams. This includes policies, access controls, bias monitoring, and

---

[7] **AI Literacy Consortium** (2025). "AI Literacy Framework Review Draft." https://ailiteracyframework.org/wp-content/uploads/2025/05/AILitFramework_ReviewDraft.pdf.

lifecycle ownership. It's often a sweet spot for product managers, data stewards, and team leads.

- **Designing AI**: Building and optimizing AI models or architectures—this is for data scientists, ML engineers, and technical roles. But even here, designing doesn't only mean coding—it includes aligning systems with human values and usability needs.

In practice, these domains can be mapped to real-world personas across your organization. Here are some examples to make it tangible:

- **Legal and compliance officer** → Managing AI: ensuring responsible and auditable usage.

- **Customer service agent** → Creating with AI: using GenAI to generate responses and summarize tickets.

- **Team lead in marketing** → Engaging with AI and Managing AI: using tools confidently while overseeing responsible rollout.

- **Data scientist or ML engineer** → Designing AI: building models, but also evaluating how users experience them.

- **Executive leadership** → All four domains: setting direction, ensuring alignment, managing risk, and guiding innovation culture.

In short, AI literacy is everyone's business, but the depth and focus change by role, which is exactly why one-size-fits-all training doesn't work. You need contextual learning that starts from use case and function, not generic slide decks.

I'll discuss AI Academies further later, but the mindset shift begins here: don't just upskill—contextualize. Embed AI thinking into everyday work, and give people time, space, and safety to experiment.

> *Literacy is not about knowing the right answer—*
> *it's about knowing how to ask better questions and judge*
> *better responses.*

AI changes how we work—but it's human competence that determines whether we thrive with it. The more accessible AI becomes, the more critical it is to help people question it, contextualize it, and yes, sometimes challenge it. AI might be the smartest tool we've ever had. But we still need to be the smartest people using it.

The full spectrum of AI technologies

Before we get into how to collaborate with AI or build trust in its outputs, we must take a step back and ensure we fully understand what we're working with. That's why this chapter exists. Even if you've read up on machine learning or played around with

ChatGPT, a refresher on the broader AI toolbox is always worth it. Because AI literacy isn't just about prompting—it's also about recognizing the difference between models that classify versus models that generate, between systems that predict versus ones that produce.

In this chapter, we'll explore some of the most prominent AI methods—both traditional and modern ones. On that note, let's take a moment to recognize the irony of calling something "traditional AI" when the whole field is younger than your career. But in enterprise language, "traditional" doesn't mean outdated—it means tested, explainable, and (mostly) reliable. And in that spirit, it's worth examining the full spectrum of AI techniques available to us today.

Traditional AI Methods

- **Supervised Learning**—You feed the model labeled data (e.g., emails marked as "spam" or "not spam") and it learns to classify new examples.

Example: Predicting customer churn or product recommendations using historical behavior.

- **Unsupervised Learning**—You let the model find patterns or groupings in data without predefined labels.

Example: Customer segmentation for marketing personalization.

- **Reinforcement Learning**—The model learns by trial and error, receiving rewards or penalties for actions.

Example: Optimizing supply chain logistics or warehouse robot movement.

- **Symbolic AI (Rule-Based Systems)**—Logic is hard-coded with "if-this-then-that" rules.

Example: Regulatory compliance checklists in banking.

- **Decision Trees and Gradient Boosting**—Algorithms that break down decisions into a series of questions based on structured input.

Example: Credit scoring or fraud detection with tabular data.

Modern AI Methods

- **Generative AI (e.g., Large Language Models like GPT)**—Models trained to generate text, images, or code based on patterns in massive datasets.

Example: AI chatbots for customer support, or text-to-image generators for marketing assets.

- **Transformers and Attention Mechanisms**—Architectures that power most state-of-the-art GenAI models.

Example: Language translation, code completion, or document summarization.

- **Multi-modal Models**—Models that can process and generate across text, image, and audio formats.

Example: AI systems that take a voice command and generate a corresponding visual.

- **Foundation Models**—Extremely large, pre-trained models that are fine-tuned for specific tasks or domains.

Example: OpenAI's GPT-4, Google's Gemini, or Meta's LLaMA for general-purpose tasks across domains.

Here's an important distinction: traditional AI models tend to be *deterministic* (not all of them are)—given the same input, they always produce the same output. This makes them easier to debug, explain, and trust. On the other hand, generative models are *probabilistic*—their output can vary even when given the same prompt, due to sampling randomness and contextual weighting.

This variability can be powerful for creativity, but dangerous when precision, consistency, or regulation is needed. That's why understanding this spectrum isn't just for your data scientists—it's a leadership-level necessity.

The biggest trap we fall into with AI is treating it like a trend rather than a toolbox. Not every problem needs GenAI. In fact, using

GenAI when it's not needed can increase cost, add unnecessary complexity, and degrade user trust.

Some problems don't require AI at all—a well-structured dashboard or a simple rules engine can often solve them more effectively. Remember, the most advanced approach is usually also the most expensive, both in terms of budget and sustainability footprint. Being mindful here is a leadership skill, not a technical constraint. Here's how traditional and generative models compare:

Characteristic	Traditional AI	Generative AI
Input	Structured data	Unstructured data (text, image, audio)
Output	Prediction, classification	Creation, synthesis
Explainability	High	Low
Stability	Deterministic	Probabilistic
Risk	More predictable	Prone to hallucinations
Best for	Forecasting, decision-making	Content creation, language interaction

Table 1: Traditional AI vs. Generative AI at a glance

Knowing what you're using and why is the first step toward AI maturity. That's why these distinctions matter so much. They can be formalized into policies, workflows, or decision guides, but they start with people understanding what tools they have at their disposal. Before scaling anything, start here. Learn the spectrum, teach your teams, and create guidelines to match the solution to the situation. That's the only way to make your AI strategy not just powerful, but useful.

Right human, right time

Oversight is often misunderstood. Especially when it comes to AI, the first reflex is usually more eyes, more people, more approvals. Throwing more humans into the loop is fun when riding rollercoasters, but it doesn't guarantee better outcomes in your AI efforts. It often just guarantees longer processes.

> *The real goal isn't to have more oversight—it's to have smarter oversight. What matters most is the right human at the right time. Not any human, not every human. The right one with the right context, expertise, or authority, embedded precisely at the moment when their judgment makes a difference.*

There's a great and well-established framework for this: the Human-in-the-Loop (HITL) design pattern. You'll find it across academic literature and practitioner models, such as the model proposed by Mosqueira-Rey, Moret-Bonillo, and Hernández-Pereira,[8] and practical guides like Google Cloud's Responsible AI recommendations.[9] And while "Human-in-the-Loop" also sounds like a brilliant name for a cereal brand, it's also a very practical architectural principle. One that's even more essential as AI

---

[8] Mosqueira-Rey, Eduardo & Hernández-Pereira, Elena & Alonso-Ríos, David & Bobes-Bascarán, José & Fernández-Leal, Ángel. (2022). Human-in-the-loop machine learning: a state of the art. Artificial Intelligence Review. 56. 10.1007/s10462-022-10246-w.

[9] https://cloud.google.com/responsible-ai.

systems become increasingly autonomous or operate across high-stakes decisions.

Let's make this concrete with two examples.

Meet Sara. She's a clinical operations specialist in a mid-sized hospital. Their AI system recommends treatment pathways based on electronic health records. However, when the system encounters rare edge cases, such as an unusual medication history or overlapping chronic conditions, these are automatically escalated to Sara for human review. She steps in, makes the call, and logs why. That feedback doesn't just improve the model's future accuracy—it ensures that oversight is meaningful, not just a box to tick.

Then there's Tom, a fraud analyst at WellBank. Any transaction flagged above €1,000 receives a quick scan from him. However, when the amount exceeds €10,000, it is routed to Lina, a senior investigator with decades of expertise. It's not just a matter of seniority—it's about criticality. Lina's judgment kicks in only where the impact could be significant. The system flows smoothly because the human attention is allocated with intent, not habit.

That's what "right human, right time" looks like in practice. And it's not just good governance—it's operationally smarter. You're avoiding unnecessary bottlenecks while still upholding accountability.

What we need are **trigger points**—well-defined moments in an AI process where human intervention is required by design, not accident. And those moments need to be owned by the people best equipped to make informed, contextual decisions. That's not always a data scientist or an engineer. Often, it's a compliance officer, a product manager, or someone with deep domain intuition who understands not just the what, but the why.

We should map oversight like we map supply chains—clearly identifying decision nodes, escalation paths, and fallback mechanisms. And we need traceability: who touched what decision, when, and why. Not for blame, but for transparency. And here's another piece many forget: oversight isn't just technical. It's emotional and political, too. People need to feel confident enough to question, pause, and say, "This isn't ready." For that, we need to cultivate the right psychological safety across our teams.

Oversight only works when people trust each other enough to step in—
and when they're trusted enough to be the ones who do.

So, next time someone says, "We need human oversight," ask, "Which human, at what point, and doing what exactly?"

Because the difference between smart oversight and inefficient friction isn't how many humans you include—it's whether you've put the right ones in the loop, at the right time. And this oversight model becomes even more critical as we move toward agentic AI (systems that act first and report later). But that's a collaboration challenge we'll tackle in Chapter 4.

Augmented intelligence

The term *augmented intelligence* sounds like a branding refresh for artificial intelligence, and in many ways, it is. However, it also reflects a subtle and critical shift in how we should approach AI in the workplace. Instead of seeing AI as a replacement for human intelligence, we can reframe it as a tool that enhances it. This human-centric perspective has been championed by thinkers like Robert S. Seiner, who described augmented intelligence in his book *Non-Invasive Data Governance Unleashed,*[10] as a way to support and enrich human decision-making rather than automate it entirely. It's a small semantic difference, but one that holds profound operational consequences.

And while we tend to focus on AI augmenting our cognitive intelligence (helping us think faster, analyze more effectively, and identify patterns), we shouldn't forget about *emotional* intelligence either. Because here's the strange twist: AI is getting good at that too.

Take Generative AI. One of its quirks is how confidently it communicates, even when it's wrong. That's because these models are designed to produce language that sounds coherent and plausible, not necessarily accurate. The result is a strange paradox: GenAI boosts your confidence while also being pliable enough to

---

[10] **Seiner, Robert S.** (2025). *Non-Invasive Data Governance Unleashed.* Technics Publications.

adapt to anything you say. That combination can be empowering or unsettling, depending on how you engage with GenAI.

But it doesn't stop at tone. A 2025 study published in *Nature* demonstrated that large language models are capable of imitating emotionally intelligent behavior, often convincingly enough to be perceived as empathetic by users.[11] That raises some big questions. Our societal definitions of emotional intelligence are constantly evolving, shaped by norms, culture, and generational change. So what happens if we start outsourcing those expressions to AI systems trained on historical patterns? Are we freezing our empathy in amber?

That's where the human role becomes even more critical. AI can suggest a compassionate response or a kind tone, but it's still on us to carry the relationship forward. Especially in contexts such as customer support, healthcare, or internal HR conversations, the distinction between simulated empathy and genuine connection remains significant.

Now let's get more practical. Augmented intelligence is already embedded into many tools we use every day, and the examples are multiplying fast. Consider digital twins, which are real-time virtual replicas of physical systems, such as wind turbines, hospital wards, or smart city infrastructure. These twins allow engineers, clinicians, and urban planners to simulate scenarios, predict

---

[11] Nature, 2024, "Large language models are proficient in solving and creating emotional intelligence tests" https://www.nature.com/articles/s44271-025-00258-x.

outcomes, and test decisions without real-world risks. Or consider co-pilot tools, such as GitHub Copilot for developers, Microsoft 365 Copilot for knowledge workers, or Salesforce Einstein Copilot for CRM teams. These systems don't replace you—they help you work faster and more confidently, leaving judgment and accountability where it belongs: with the human.

The key to all of this is context.

These systems work best when we prompt them with clear intent, interpret their output with informed judgment, and know when to step in. That's why we need to stay in the driver's seat—letting AI steer with us, but never letting go of the wheel.

Now, let's not forget that there's a dark side to this, too. The more we lean on AI to "sound smart" or "feel human," the easier it becomes to disengage our own critical thinking. That's especially true with GenAI, which can sound so helpful that we stop questioning it. That's why augmented intelligence also means being mindful of our role—to interpret, to redirect, and to challenge the system when necessary.

So here's the final call to action: if we want AI to augment our work, not automate or distort it, then we need to embed that philosophy into everything we do. That means running AI training sessions that reinforce augmentation over automation, defining policies that clearly outline the human role, and communicating effectively across teams that humans remain the primary decision-makers. Because augmentation isn't just a technology choice—it's a mindset. And that mindset is what keeps us human.

Confidence

There's something strange about the way AI speaks. You've probably noticed it too. The tone, the rhythm, the flow—it sounds so sure of itself. Generative AI, in particular, has mastered the art of confidence. It answers questions with conviction, wraps uncertainty in persuasive language, and gives you exactly what you asked for in a tone that makes you second-guess what you initially thought. And that's where the problem begins.

The paradox here is powerful and subtle. When a machine responds confidently, it can either make us feel more confident or less. For some, the AI's composure is reassuring and empowering. For others, especially when the AI contradicts their intuition or expertise, it sparks doubt. This isn't just a theoretical concern. Researchers at the MIT Media Lab conducted a study in which participants asked GPT-style models to solve reasoning tasks, and the results showed that users who relied on the AI tended to perform worse than those who reasoned on their own. The researchers titled the paper *"Your Brain on ChatGPT"*[12] and its conclusion was clear:

Relying too much on confident AI erodes critical thinking.

This isn't just about logic. It's about psychology. Confidence and competence are not always aligned in human minds, and AI amplifies that misalignment. Think about the Dunning-Kruger effect, where people with low ability overestimate their own competence.[13] Now add AI into that equation: a confident-sounding assistant that gives you plausible answers in a blink. The risk? People stop verifying, stop learning, and start assuming correctness by tone.

On the other side, we have imposter syndrome. The nagging sense that "I don't belong here" or "I'm not good enough," even when the evidence says otherwise. First described by Clance and Imes in 1978,[14] it's a common struggle—especially in high-performing environments. And now we're adding AI into the mix. Imagine what it does to your confidence when the tool you're supposed to

---

[12] MIT Media Lab, 2024, https://www.media.mit.edu/publications/your-brain-on-chatgpt.

[13] Kruger J, Dunning D. Unskilled and unaware of it: how difficulties in recognizing one's own incompetence lead to inflated self-assessments. J Pers Soc Psychol. 1999 Dec;77(6):1121-34. doi: 10.1037//0022-3514.77.6.1121. PMID: 10626367.

[14] Clance, P. R., & Imes, S. A. (1978). The imposter phenomenon in high achieving women: Dynamics and therapeutic intervention. Psychotherapy: Theory, Research & Practice, 15(3), 241–247. https://doi.org/10.1037/h0086006.

collaborate with always seems to have a smarter, faster answer. Suddenly, people hesitate to speak up, even when the AI is obviously wrong.

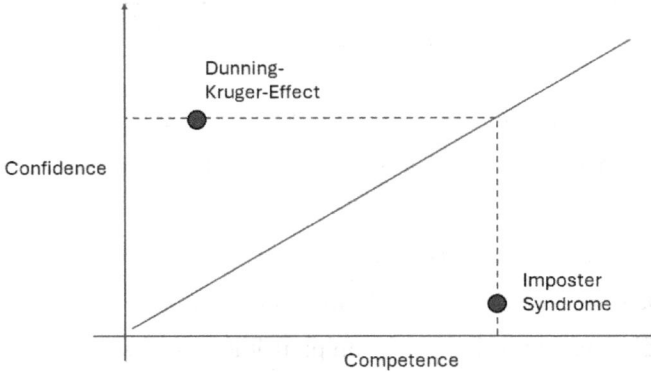

Figure 3: Confidence vs. Competence.

This is where the real work begins. Organizations need to think of AI not just as a knowledge engine, but as a tone engine. The way AI speaks influences how we think. That means designing AI experiences—especially internal tools—to be aware of their tone impact. Give users cues to stay engaged in critical thinking. And most importantly, normalize the idea that double-checking AI is not a sign of distrust—it's a sign of strength.

One way to reinforce this is through prompt design and output review. Conduct internal audits to see whether AI-generated content inadvertently inflates confidence. Another approach is to create safe spaces where employees can express concerns when they feel either too dependent or too uncertain due to AI outputs. This can be part of AI onboarding, documentation, or even regular retrospectives in teams that actively use AI.

> *Confidence, ultimately, is not just a feeling. It's a shared state between humans and the systems we work with. And if we don't actively shape that relationship, we risk building tools that undermine our people instead of empowering them.*

Adaptive curiosity

If there's one human trait that AI can't replace, but can either strengthen or suppress, it's curiosity. Our ability to ask questions, explore the unknown, and stay open to possibilities is what drives meaningful change. But curiosity doesn't always come naturally in organizations. Especially when the pressure is high, time is short, and AI promises to deliver answers faster than we can even formulate the questions.

Adaptive curiosity[15] is about staying inquisitive even in the face of overwhelming certainty or complexity. It's not just about wondering, "What can this new model do?" but "What problem are we trying to solve?" and "What would happen if we didn't use AI here at all?"

In practical terms, curiosity often determines whether an AI initiative becomes transformative or just another tool collecting dust. But for that to happen, we need to move curiosity beyond

---

[15] Schmidhuber, J. (1991). Adaptive confidence and adaptive curiosity. Forschungsberichte, TU Munich, FKI 149 91, 1-9.

the philosophical and into the practical: it must become a business skill. The best AI use cases don't emerge from rigid playbooks—they come from teams who are encouraged to question existing processes, experiment with new workflows, and challenge the status quo. That's why curiosity should be baked into KPIs, hiring criteria, and even post-mortem discussions.

For example:

- Did we ask "What if?" enough during the pilot?

- What questions were raised, but not answered, during implementation?

- Who asked a question that changed our direction?

There's also a neuroscience angle here. Research shows that curiosity literally activates reward centers in the brain, specifically the dopaminergic system and the hippocampus, which is responsible for learning and memory.[16] This is not just metaphorical—it's biological. Adaptive curiosity is our brain's natural antidote to fear-based stagnation. It replaces paralysis with possibility.

---

[16] Gruber, Matthias & Gelman, Bernard & Ranganath, Charan. (2014). States of Curiosity Modulate Hippocampus-Dependent Learning via the Dopaminergic Circuit. Neuron. 84. 10.1016/j.neuron.2014.08.060.

Organizations can design for this. IDEO, for example, builds curiosity into its design sprints as a core input.[17] Some AI-forward companies host internal "question jams" or allow experimentation weeks where people can explore new ideas without needing permission or budget pre-approval. When teams have to justify every idea before they're allowed to try it, curiosity dies quietly. To make adaptive curiosity part of your culture, you could:

- Celebrate good questions during retrospectives, not just successful answers.

- Allocate time in meetings for "What if?" exploration.

- Add curiosity metrics to performance reviews, such as cross-functional explorations, use case ideation, or knowledge sharing.

- Design AI onboarding to include not only what the tools do, but also what they don't.

In the age of AI, it's easy to feel like we're supposed to have all the answers. But the leaders and teams that will thrive aren't the ones with all the answers. They're the ones who stay committed to asking better questions.

---

[17] IDEO. (2017, November 16). *What are the top 5 behaviors of design-driven organizations and why do they matter?* IDEO Design Thinking Blog. https://designthinking.ideo.com/blog/what-are-the-top-5-behaviors-of-design-driven-organizations-and-why-do-they-matter.

Adapting to AI-relevant roles

If there's one truth about working with AI, it's this: no single role has all the answers. The people building AI aren't always the ones deploying it. The people governing AI aren't always the ones using it. And the people benefiting from AI might not even realize what's under the hood. That's why the idea of "wearing different hats" isn't just a metaphor—it's a survival skill.

In my previous book on data strategy, I introduced a list of these metaphorical hats—personas we shift between depending on the challenge at hand. For AI, this list still holds, but some new roles have entered the room. Translator. Architect. Visionary. These aren't buzzwords—they're reflections of the very real ways AI is reshaping decision-making, alignment, and delivery.

Each hat represents a particular kind of contribution. Such as, a:

- Therapist helps teams manage change and emotional resistance.
- Project Manager ensures structure and delivery in AI experimentation.
- Negotiator balances trade-offs between accuracy and explainability.
- Detective investigates unexpected outcomes and model behavior.
- Communicator translates AI complexity into human insight.
- Developer brings technical feasibility into focus.

- Diplomat balances compliance, privacy, and business needs.
- Translator bridges business needs and model capabilities.
- Domain Expert brings grounding to data assumptions.
- Visionary sees the long-term implications and new frontiers.
- Architect connects AI to infrastructure, data, and governance.

To make this more tangible, here's a table mapping each hat to a situation, objective, and required skillset:

	Situation (Example)	Objective	Skills to Apply
Therapist	Resistance to AI tool rollout	Build emotional safety, reduce fear	Empathy, change management
Project Manager	AI pilot in execution	Ensure timely and aligned delivery	Coordination, milestone tracking
Negotiator	Conflict over explainability vs accuracy	Find the balance, align stakeholders	Listening, trade-off framing
Detective	Model behavior is off	Trace errors, surface root cause	Data literacy, model knowledge
Communicator	Execs want to understand impact	Simplify and humanize complexity	Storytelling, business alignment
Developer	Building proof-of-concept	Prototype fast and safe	Coding, ML knowledge
Diplomat	GDPR compliance in AI feature design	Respect regulation while delivering value	Legal fluency, boundary work
Translator	Business problem to model design	Ensure AI solves the right problem	Prompting, abstraction, systems thinking

	Situation (Example)	Objective	Skills to Apply
Domain Expert	Reviewing training data	Confirm relevance and accuracy	Field expertise, context awareness
Visionary	AI Council planning for future roles	Map new opportunities and threats	Strategic foresight, humility
Architect	Connecting AI model to enterprise systems	Build scalable, secure AI infrastructure	Platform knowledge, integration mindset

Table 2: Different hats to wear when working with AI

It's not about wearing all hats at once. It's about being conscious of which one you need to wear in a given moment and, more importantly, when to take it off. Wearing the wrong hat can be more than awkward—it can lead to misunderstandings, poor decisions, or unproductive tension. Imagine an AI ethics discussion where someone shows up wearing the Developer hat, focused only on performance metrics. Or a governance workshop where the Project Manager dominates, rushing to conclusions before risks are surfaced. Right hats, wrong context.

Let me give you three quick stories:

Elena, an AI Product Manager, starts her day aligning a new GenAI-powered assistant with marketing leads, wearing the Communicator hat to explain why hallucinations still happen. In the afternoon, she's troubleshooting training data skew, slipping into the Detective hat to guide her team through the audit.

Dev, a senior compliance officer, has to evaluate whether an open-source model violates IP policies. He's not a lawyer, but he switches into the Diplomat hat, listening to legal, security, and engineering teams to form a position that protects the company without killing innovation.

Lisa, a business lead launching a customer service chatbot, starts as a Visionary, mapping new ways to interact. But when her chatbot starts giving financial advice, she scrambles to put on the Project Manager hat to shut it down, reassess, and get cross-functional input fast.

These hats aren't fixed roles—they're adaptive stances. And that's what makes them powerful. But they're also incomplete without context. This is where Laura Madsen's description of the Sustainable Disruption Model[18] becomes incredibly useful. Madsen outlines three persona types in relation to change, applied specifically to AI transformation:

- Disrupters find comfort in change and often initiate it.

- Optimizers like to take existing things and improve them.

- Keepers enjoy keeping the status quo and "keeping the lights on."

You can see how these archetypes align with the hats above. A Visionary might be a Disrupter. A Project Manager typically plays the role of the Optimizer. A Diplomat—clearly a Keeper.

---

[18] **Madsen, Laura** (2024). *AI and the Data Revolution*. Technics Publications.

Recognizing who tends to wear what and who is missing from the table is a huge part of AI strategy.

If we're going to make AI a value driver across the enterprise, we need to match the right skills to the right hats—and ensure people have the psychological safety and structural permission to wear them. That means including these roles in job descriptions. Asking about them in one-on-one meetings and celebrating them in performance reviews.

Wearing different hats isn't just a survival tactic—it's a strategy. One that ensures the people behind the AI are just as adaptive as the models they build.

Building learning ecosystems for AI maturity

When it comes to AI upskilling efforts, most organizations are still stuck in a dated learning model: one-off training sessions, certifications that appear impressive on paper, or slide decks gathering dust. But AI doesn't wait for quarterly upskilling initiatives—it moves fast, and if we want to keep up, our learning ecosystems need to do the same.

AI maturity isn't a destination you reach by attending a workshop. It's something that needs to be built into the workflow. Think smart nudges embedded in your tools. Microlearning occurs when you're performing the task. Feedback loops make your AI interactions better. It's not about building a course—it's about creating a culture that doesn't stop learning.

And here's the twist: AI itself can help us learn not just in the abstract, but in really practical ways. Imagine personalized learning paths shaped by your job function. Real-time coaching when you're working with AI tools. Simulated decision-making environments where you can safely explore edge cases, like customer complaints, ethical dilemmas, or policy enforcement scenarios, without the real-world consequences.

However, none of this works if people are afraid to appear "dumb" by asking questions. That's why psychological safety is the foundation of any serious AI learning culture. If you want people to challenge AI outputs, spot hallucinations, or push back on automated decisions, they need to know they won't be punished for speaking up. We need to stop treating uncertainty as a sign of incompetence. In fact, the best AI collaborators are often the ones asking the hardest questions.

So, how do you build a real learning ecosystem around AI? Start by bringing people together. Pair up AI-savvy team members with domain experts in reverse (or is it forward? Sideways?) mentoring arrangements. Host collaborative labs where people try tools, test edge cases, and share what worked (or didn't). Build communities of practice around AI topics, and let those communities run with their own rhythm, language, and rituals.

Then make learning discoverable. Use retrieval-augmented generation (RAG) setups - essentially AI that can search through your organization's actual documents and knowledge before answering - to power internal Q&A tools. Let people search for what others have tried, failed at, and learned from. Utilize your own AI to assist your team in learning about AI.

If you really want to go big—and I think you should—establish an internal AI Academy. You may remember the concept from the Data Academy we discussed in *Humanizing Data Strategy*. The idea is similar here: create a dedicated space for hands-on education, peer learning, and team-based exploration. Add gamification to the mix—points, badges, challenges, friendly competition—and suddenly you've turned upskilling from a compliance activity into a movement.

Building AI capability in your organization is not just about installing tools—it's about building learning loops. Make learning visible. Make it social. And most importantly, make it continuous.

Gamification

Gamification has always been a powerful way to incentivize behaviors in organizations. From earning airline miles to finishing e-learning modules, humans respond well to progress bars, badges, and a little healthy competition. When done right, gamification taps into our intrinsic motivations—curiosity, mastery, status, and a sense of belonging. That's why it's an excellent tool to make AI adoption less intimidating and more engaging. We already touched on this briefly in the context of AI Academies—gamification created a natural sense of progression and peer learning.

However, gamification isn't just a tool for teaching people about AI. Increasingly, it's also how we *teach AI* itself. Some of the most significant breakthroughs in AI came from gaming. Remember when AlphaZero rewrote the rules of chess and Go by playing against itself millions of times?[19] Or how reinforcement learning agents are trained by mastering video games like Breakout[20] and StarCraft?[21] Games provide bounded environments with clear rules and feedback loops—ideal conditions for machines to learn complex strategies. Even recent experiments have shown that AI

---

[19] David Silver et al. ,A general reinforcement learning algorithm that masters chess, shogi, and Go through self-play.Science362,1140-1144(2018).DOI:10.1126/science.aar6404.

[20] **Mnih, V., Kavukcuoglu, K., Silver, D., et al. (2015).** *Human-level control through deep reinforcement learning.* **Nature, 518**, 529–533. https://doi.org/10.1038/nature14236.

[21] **Vinyals, O., Babuschkin, I., Czarnecki, W. M., et al. (2019).** *Grandmaster level in StarCraft II using multi-agent reinforcement learning.* **Nature, 575**, 350–354. https://doi.org/10.1038/s41586-019-1724-z.

can learn mathematical reasoning by playing Snake or Tetris-like environments.[22]

That creates a fascinating feedback loop. Gamification is used to teach AI, and AI can, in turn, use gamification to teach humans. For example, AI-powered onboarding tools can utilize scenario-based challenges to instruct employees on how to interact responsibly with generative tools. Learning modules can dynamically adjust to a person's strengths and weaknesses, offering just the right challenge to keep them engaged. This isn't theoretical—it's already happening in training platforms, simulation environments, and upskilling tools being deployed across various industries.

One additional dimension worth calling out is how gamification can also be used by AI to subtly optimize human behavior. Drawing from the behavioral economics theory of *nudges*[23] (gentle, indirect suggestions that influence decision-making), we can apply these principles in AI-driven systems. For example, an AI co-pilot could nudge an analyst to double-check a prompt that might lead to misleading output, or recommend a more inclusive phrasing in communication. These small adjustments, delivered in gameful ways, reinforce desired behaviors without overwhelming users.

---

[22] https://the-decoder.de/ki-modell-lernt-mathematisches-denken-durch-snake-und-tetris-aehnliche-spiele/.

[23] Thaler, R. H., & Sunstein, C. R. (2012). *Nudge: The Final Edition*. Penguin.

When applied thoughtfully, gamification is not motivational fluff—it's a serious lever to accelerate learning, reinforce habits, and build meaningful relationships between people and machines. And it's fun. Which is something we could all use a little more of, especially when working with technology that still feels a bit like science fiction.

That's also why we should treat gamification not just as a learning tool, but as a strategic lever. If you're trying to embed AI into your organization in a meaningful way, gamification gives you a concrete mechanism to nudge the right behaviors, encourage exploration, and make progress visible. Whether your goal is to increase AI adoption, improve data quality for AI models, or develop responsible usage habits across teams, there's a gamified way to do it. Gamification is how we operationalize our AI strategy in ways that are human, scalable, and impactful.

Future career paths around AI

If you're wondering whether your job will survive the AI wave, you're not alone. But maybe that's the wrong question. A more helpful one might be: How will your job evolve because of AI? Whether we like it or not, AI is reshaping every job, not necessarily replacing it, but reframing what it means to do that job well.

What we're seeing is a realignment of responsibilities. Repetitive, routine tasks, such as scheduling, summarizing, and document drafting, are increasingly being offloaded to machines. That doesn't make your role less important. It makes it more focused. The work that remains tends to be more strategic, more interpersonal, or more nuanced—the kind of work where humans are still uniquely good. But that shift doesn't happen by itself. It requires conscious redesign, reskilling, and, most importantly, a mindset that's open to change.

In many ways, AI is pushing us to be more human, not less. That means investing in what I'd call AI-adjacent skills, such as critical thinking, ethical reasoning, communication, and the ability to ask better questions. It also means embracing new types of roles. One category gaining ground fast is what we might call AI-enabling roles—jobs that focus on selecting, guiding, fine-tuning, or overseeing AI tools. These aren't just data science positions. They include domain experts who validate AI outputs, legal professionals who ensure regulatory alignment, and project managers who orchestrate AI delivery without ever needing to touch code.

In fact, we're already seeing a wave of new job titles emerge that reflect this shift, such as:

- AI Product Managers understanding both technology and human impact.

- Prompt Engineers and AI Trainers fine-tuning models and instructions.

- Ethics Leads specializing in responsible AI design.

- AI Translators bridging business needs and technical teams.

We're also seeing the rise of AI-literate leaders—executives and team leads who don't build models, but understand their implications, limitations, and risks. These are the people who know enough to ask the right questions, translate technical insights into business actions, and guide their organizations toward responsible innovation. As Pascal Bornet writes in *Irreplaceable: How Humans Will Remain Essential in the AI Era* (Wiley, 2023), the most future-ready professionals will be "AI-ready, human-ready, and change-ready." These qualities will show up in job descriptions more and more, either explicitly or between the lines.

Being "change-ready" isn't just about acquiring new technical skills. It's about building emotional agility—staying curious, open, and resilient in the face of evolving demands. That's harder than it sounds, especially when the ground beneath you keeps shifting. But it's also where the opportunity lies.

And here's where it ties directly to AI strategy: You can't design an AI strategy in a vacuum, as if people were static building blocks. Strategy depends on capability. And capability depends on who is in the room, and how ready they are to evolve. If you're defining an AI strategy today and not considering how roles are changing, how people learn, and how future skills will be built, then you're not really designing a strategy, you're just making a wish list. Talent and capability are part of the infrastructure. And no model, however advanced, can succeed if the humans around it aren't empowered to guide, govern, and grow with it.

So what does this mean for you, practically speaking? It means adopting new habits. Start by learning how to prompt and critique AI tools. Stay close to the real-world use cases that are emerging in your field. Don't just marvel at what's possible—understand what's practical, what's ethical, and what's useful. Take the time to ask how AI can make your work better—not just faster.

If you're in a position of influence, don't leave your teams to figure this out on their own. Create safe spaces to experiment. Offer coaching, training, or new learning paths. Help people reimagine their roles, rather than fearing for them. Whether you're writing job descriptions, facilitating performance reviews, or mapping out future teams, you are shaping what the future of work with AI will look like.

That future isn't pre-written. It's not hard-coded. It's co-created by all of us who are willing to evolve, together.

"Together" is a great keyword to segue into the next chapter, where we discuss collaboration in all shapes and forms that working with AI enables nowadays. So let's keep going.

Four

Collaboration

Collaboration has always been essential, but AI is forcing us to rethink what it truly means to work together, not just between teams or departments, but between human beings and intelligent systems. That shift changes everything. It's no longer enough to simply discuss teamwork or cross-functional cooperation in the same way we have always. Because AI isn't just another tool in the workflow—it's a new kind of colleague, assistant, or sometimes even decision-maker.

The myth of the lone genius has long been outdated. Real breakthroughs—especially the ones that stick—come from complex, messy, interdisciplinary effort. In the age of AI, that effort is no longer purely human. The most innovative teams today are often hybrid teams: a mix of domain experts, technical specialists, and now, machine counterparts. That changes how we brainstorm, how we delegate, and how we trust.

And trust is where things get interesting. Because collaboration is not just about tasks, it's about relationships, rituals, and responsibilities. When AI enters the picture, those things shift. Suddenly, we're asking: Who gets the final say? What does accountability look like when a machine does half the work? What kind of communication do we need across these new boundaries?

This chapter is about these questions. It's about redefining collaboration—not as a static structure, but as a living system that adapts to the presence of AI. We'll explore the new team dynamics that emerge when AI becomes part of the team, the cultural and organizational shifts required, and how to build collaborative environments where people and machines not only coexist but actually thrive together.

Co-creation over coordination

If you've worked on any AI initiative recently, you've probably noticed that the traditional way of collaborating just doesn't cut it anymore. The old handoff model, where data gets prepared by one team, passed to another for modeling, then handed off again for business deployment, is too slow, too siloed, and frankly too risky for what AI demands. That approach might have worked (barely) for business intelligence dashboards, but with AI, the stakes are higher, the timelines are tighter, and the margins for misunderstanding are razor-thin.

That's why co-creation needs to replace coordination. And I don't just mean inviting a business stakeholder to a steering committee meeting once a month. I mean actual, structured, ongoing collaboration—where data experts, AI developers, business users, domain specialists, compliance officers, and end users are involved early and often, not just at the end. In *Humanizing Data Strategy*, I described co-creation as a healthy mindset in any operating model, whether you're running a central service or supporting decentralized, self-service teams. For AI, this mindset is equally, and maybe even more, important. As soon as we begin automating decisions or scaling customer interactions, we must ensure that the system reflects not only technical feasibility but also real-world usability, relevance, and accountability.

Now, I usually don't get too caught up philosophizing about definitions, but in this case, it's worth taking a moment to get specific. Because the term "co-creation" is often misunderstood or watered down. It's not the same as a transaction, where one team gives requirements and the other delivers a product or a service. And it's not the same as coordination, where multiple parties keep each other updated, but still operate in silos. Co-creation implies shared ownership throughout the process. And it rests on three specific ingredients:

- **Shared Purpose**—Everyone involved is aiming for the same outcome, not pushing their own agendas.

Example: A compliance officer and an ML engineer working together to build explainability into a credit scoring model, not debating whose priorities matter more.

- **Clear Contributions**—Each role brings specific expertise and knows when and how to apply it.

Example: A domain expert validating model output assumptions before a solution is shipped, rather than reviewing it post-launch.

- **Formal Commitment**—Co-creation needs structure, not just goodwill.

Example: Having a jointly defined working agreement or charter that outlines who does what, when, and how decisions are made.

Let me tell you a story—maybe one that feels uncomfortably familiar. Picture a company trying to build an AI-powered customer support bot. The data team prepared the chat logs. The AI team fine-tuned the model. The product owner scheduled the release. Everything seemed ready. But no one involved the frontline support agents until a week before launch. The bot answered questions in ways that sounded confident but were completely off-base—using internal slang, referencing outdated policies, and misinterpreting tone. Customers were confused, support tickets spiked, and internal trust eroded. The project didn't fail because the model was bad. It failed because co-creation didn't happen.

Now imagine the same scenario—but this time, support agents are brought in early to tag helpful responses, flag confusing language, and help define success criteria. Compliance reviews the model for edge cases, and leadership agrees on a shared outcome that extends beyond simply reducing ticket volume. That's co-creation. And that's what makes AI projects not just more inclusive, but more successful.

Co-creation is messy. It requires facilitation, a shared vocabulary, and sometimes considerable patience. But it's also the fastest route to clarity. When you incorporate diverse perspectives into the design process from the outset, you identify blind spots before they become risks. You build context into the system, not as a patch later on but as part of the foundation. You create shared ownership, which leads to better adoption, stronger buy-in, and fewer backtracking issues after go-live.

This doesn't mean every AI project needs a dozen cooks in the kitchen. It means designing with the right people in the room, at the right time, with clearly defined roles. It also means treating AI projects not just as technical implementations, but as socio-technical systems that blend human insight with machine capability. In that context, co-creation isn't just a nice-to-have—it's the only way to make sure the solution you build fits the problem you're trying to solve.

Federated governance for AI using autonomy and alignment

If working with AI was playing football, then AI strategy would be the coach giving the direction, and AI governance would be the referee to make sure everyone sticks to the rules and plays nice. You can't win without a game plan—but you also can't play fair without rules, boundaries, and someone making sure they're respected. That's the role federated governance plays in the world of enterprise AI.

The moment AI became self-service, governance had to evolve. Unlike traditional software deployments that go through a central IT pipeline, modern AI tools, especially GenAI platforms, are often directly accessible by teams and individuals across the organization. It's easier than ever to spin up a model, connect a chatbot, or test a proof of concept in a sandbox environment. And while that's exciting, it's also risky.

Because when experimentation happens everywhere, oversight can't happen anywhere.

That's where federated governance comes in. It's the middle ground between complete centralization where every AI use case is reviewed and approved by a single group, and chaotic decentralization where anything goes. Governance isn't about control—it's about collaboration. In the context of AI, this collaboration must reflect the diverse maturity levels, use cases, and ambitions that different teams bring to the table.

A federated model enables business units to experiment and innovate while maintaining alignment with core principles, including ethics, compliance, data privacy, and platform consistency. It accepts that not all teams are at the same level of AI readiness—and that's okay. What matters is that the guardrails are clear and the responsibilities are shared. It also reinforces that AI governance isn't just the job of data scientists or legal departments. It's a shared commitment across functions.

So what does this look like in practice? Here's one way to organize federated AI governance:

- **AI Strategy Board**—Sets the overall direction for AI use, including long-term priorities, ethical principles, and alignment to business goals. Usually composed of C-level leadership, risk management, and strategic tech leaders.

- **AI Review Council**—A cross-functional body that evaluates high-impact or sensitive use cases, especially those involving personal data, fairness concerns, or external exposure. Their job is to spot red flags and elevate unresolved risks.

- **AI Product Owners**—Individuals responsible for delivering and managing specific AI systems or applications. They work closely with users and ensure that models or agents are iteratively improved, not just launched and forgotten.

- **AI Stewards**—These are the local champions embedded within business units. They keep a close eye on day-to-day AI use, help teams navigate governance frameworks, and act as the bridge between centralized guidance and real-world execution.

- **AI Operations & Monitoring Team**—Focuses on technical monitoring, including performance drift, anomaly detection, retraining cycles, and usage audits. They're the ones ensuring that what was deployed last quarter continues to perform safely today.

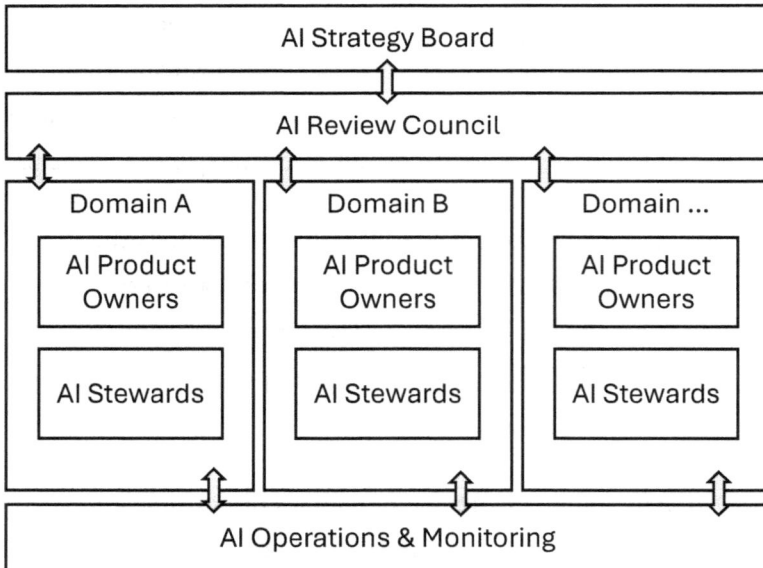

Figure 4: Governance Organization as Example.

Let me give you a quick (fictional) example. *At Syntria Health, a growing diagnostics company, the cardiology department built its own GenAI-based assistant to summarize patient notes. It worked—until one output confused a mild allergy with a life-threatening one. That triggered a formal review, and instead of shutting the tool down, the AI Review Council engaged with the team. Together, they embedded an AI steward in the cardiology unit, added performance monitoring, and revised the prompt logic. The result? Not only did the assistant get approved, but it also became the model for decentralized AI use in other departments.*

This structure mirrors the trajectory that data governance once followed. Back then, we saw a similar move away from rigid central models toward more adaptive, federated structures. With AI, the complexity is higher, but the need is the same: let people build, but build safely.

The parallels run deeper than just structure. Both data governance and AI governance wrestle with the same fundamental tensions: innovation versus control, speed versus safety, local context versus enterprise consistency. Both require translating technical complexity into business language that executives can act on. Both depend on people who might not have "governance" in their title, caring about governance in their daily work. And perhaps most importantly, both fail spectacularly when treated as purely technical exercises. The lessons learned from data governance— that policies need to be living documents, that culture eats compliance for breakfast, that you need both carrots and sticks— all apply directly to AI governance. The main difference? AI governance must address systems that can act autonomously, make decisions in milliseconds, and produce outputs that are convincing, even when they're completely wrong. It's as if data governance has grown up, earned a PhD, and developed some concerning habits that we need to keep an eye on.

You can't govern what you don't understand.

Federated AI governance only works when everyone involved, from legal to operations to engineering, has at least a baseline AI literacy. It's not about turning everyone into a data scientist. It's about enabling informed judgment, asking better questions, and spotting the risks that technology alone can't. Because when governance is everyone's job, AI becomes everyone's opportunity.

When AI takes initiative

When we talk about collaboration in organizations, we usually mean between people. Cross-functional teams, interdisciplinary squads, agile workflows—all of it relies on the messy but beautiful art of human collaboration. But with AI stepping into the room, that equation starts to change. The question is no longer just "How do we work with each other?" but also "How do we work with the machines that now shape, support, and sometimes steer our decisions?"

In his book *Co-Intelligence,*[24] Ethan Mollick gives us a useful lens. He describes three different relationships people have with AI: co-worker, co-teacher, and coach. These aren't metaphors—they reflect how people are actually treating AI in the wild. Sometimes we hand off tasks to AI like a diligent intern. Sometimes we ask it to explain things like a patient tutor. And sometimes, we even let it guide our thinking like a trusted mentor. These are fundamentally different ways of relating to a machine—and they raise big questions for how we design, deploy, and govern AI in the workplace.

What makes this even more interesting—and complicated—is that these relationships aren't uniform. Different people experience AI in other ways, depending on their personality, technical confidence, emotional needs, or even how their AI tool responds to them. One employee might treat their AI assistant like a helpful sidekick. Another might rely on it for validation. A third might avoid it entirely. These relationships evolve, just like human ones. Which means your organization doesn't have a single "relationship with AI"—it has hundreds or thousands of micro-relationships, each with its own dynamics.

And these dynamics are only getting more complex with the rise of agentic AI, generate plans, or even take action on behalf of users. This isn't just a technical evolution—it's a fundamental shift in how collaboration works. When your AI colleague starts the conversation instead of waiting for you to ask, everything changes.

---

[24] **Mollick, Ethan** (2023). *Co-Intelligence: Living and Working with AI.*

Suddenly, you're not managing a tool; you're managing a relationship with something that has its own kind of initiative.

Think about the psychological impact of that shift. For decades, we've been the ones in charge—we open the software, we click the buttons, we initiate every interaction. But when AI starts suggesting tasks you didn't think of, flagging issues you missed, or even completing work while you were in another meeting, it can feel unsettling. Some people find it liberating—finally, a partner that's always thinking ahead! Others find it invasive or even threatening. "Why is it making suggestions I didn't ask for?" "Does it think I'm not doing my job well enough?" These aren't technical questions—they're deeply human reactions to a changing power dynamic.

This shift has created entirely new collaboration patterns. We're moving from "human as initiator" to "human as reviewer"—from driving every action to quality-checking actions the AI has already taken. Instead of asking "What should we analyze?" we're increasingly asking "Is this analysis the AI produced correct?" Instead of writing from scratch, we're editing and refining. Instead of searching for opportunities, we're evaluating the opportunities the AI surfaced. It's a bit like moving from being a chef to being a food critic—both require expertise, but they're fundamentally different roles.

This volatility is unevenly distributed across teams. Some departments embrace AI as a productivity partner. Others resist it as a threat. Some leaders want AI to accelerate decision-making.

Others worry about losing control. And in the absence of clear expectations, AI becomes whatever each person thinks it is, which leads to misalignment, inconsistent results, and sometimes, chaos.

That's why collaboration models need to be part of AI strategy— not as an afterthought, but as a core design decision. We need to decide and communicate what kind of collaborator AI is meant to be in a given context. Is it a proactive assistant that should surface opportunities? A reactive tool that only responds when asked? Something in between? These aren't just design choices—they're cultural statements about how work gets done and who's in charge.

Informally, organizations need to get curious. How are people talking to AI? What do they expect from it? When does it help, and when does it confuse or frustrate? How do they feel when AI initiates rather than responds? These aren't just UX questions. They're cultural questions.

How we relate to technology shapes how we relate to our work, and to each other.

And let's be honest for a moment: human relationships are already complicated enough. So, I wouldn't be surprised if, a few years from now, we start seeing companies hire AI-human mediators or facilitators—maybe even couples' therapists—to resolve tension between a team and their increasingly assertive chatbots. It sounds absurd until you realize it's already happening in subtle ways. Teams blame AI for bad decisions, praise it for good ones, and sometimes argue over whether the tool is "smart" or "broken." That's not tool usage—that's relationship dynamics.

To help organizations navigate this space, there are some great frameworks to draw from:

- **Sociotechnical Systems Theory**[25] reminds us that we have to optimize both the technical and the human parts of a system, not just one or the other.

- **Responsible Innovation**[26] encourages us to embed societal and ethical reflection into the development of new capabilities, not bolt it on later.

- **Scenario Planning**[27] gives us a way to imagine divergent futures—where AI plays a small, supportive role or becomes a dominant force—and make sure our strategies hold up across those possibilities.

So what does that look like in practice? It means building rituals and feedback loops that surface how AI is actually used and experienced, not just how it's intended to be. It means creating

---

[25] Pasmore, W., Winby, S., Mohrman, S. A., & Vanasse, R. (2018). Reflections: Sociotechnical Systems Design and Organization Change. *Journal of Change Management, 19*(2), 67–85. https://doi.org/10.1080/14697017.2018.1553761.

[26] Stilgoe, J., Owen, R., & Macnaghten, P. (2013). *Developing a framework for responsible innovation.* Research Policy, 42(9), 1568-1580.

[27] Schoemaker, P. J. H. (1995). *Scenario Planning: A Tool for Strategic Thinking.* Sloan Management Review, 36(2), 25-40.

safe spaces for teams to discuss their comfort, discomfort, and confusion with AI tools, especially when AI begins to take the initiative. It means including collaboration modes in strategic documents: Is AI meant to suggest, assist, or act in this workflow? And when it acts, what's the human's role—validator, editor, or observer? Most importantly, it means treating collaboration with AI as a skill—something that can be taught, developed, and improved over time.

> *We need to take our relationships with AI seriously—*
> *not because AI has feelings, but because we do.*

How we feel about AI will shape how we use it, trust it, and ultimately, how successful we are in working with it. Whether AI waits for our command or jumps in with suggestions, whether we're initiators or reviewers, whether we're leading or following— these aren't just technical configurations. They're choices about what kind of future we're building, one interaction at a time.

Cross-functional by default

When building AI systems within an organization, the technology is rarely the most challenging part. What's hard is alignment. AI systems often fall apart not because the models are wrong, but because the teams around them were never aligned in the first place. Different incentives, different vocabularies, different assumptions about what "success" looks like—these are the real blockers.

That's why cross-functional collaboration is non-negotiable. I don't mean holding a big kickoff call and hoping for the best for everyone. I mean truly multidisciplinary teams—legal, security, ethics, business, tech—working together from day one. Not in parallel. Not in sequence. But together. Designing, building, testing, challenging, and evolving the system as one unit.

We've seen what happens when this doesn't happen. Models that get built and never deployed because the business team wasn't consulted. Legal teams brought in a week before go-live, only to flag major issues that could have been resolved months earlier. Governance teams are scrambling to retrofit policies after the fact. It's not that anyone is slacking off—it's that they weren't in the room early enough.

Domain experts, for instance, aren't just "nice to have." They're essential for validating outputs, flagging misinterpretations, and providing the nuance that raw data or algorithms can't detect. On the other side, technical teams need the business and ethical context to avoid optimizing for the wrong signals. We've all seen well-trained models that optimize for KPIs that look great on paper but fail to deliver in real life.

The solution isn't just more meetings. It's structured collaboration. It's shared vocabularies and working agreements.

A helpful reference here is the book "Team Topologies" by Matthew Skelton and Manuel Pais (IT Revolution Press, 2019). They introduce team patterns like stream-aligned teams, enabling teams, and complicated subsystem teams—and while it's not an AI book, the principles absolutely apply. For example, enabling teams can act as internal consultants or accelerators for AI adoption, helping other groups build capability without assuming full ownership of outcomes. In AI contexts, that could mean an MLOps (short for Machine Learning Operations) enabling team or an ethics working group that supports product squads.

What's important is to design your collaboration model explicitly. Don't just say, "We need legal involved." Say when and how. Will they be part of sprint planning? Do they have veto power? Are there pre-agreed triggers for review? Clarity beats ambiguity every time.

If you're developing your AI strategy, this needs to be baked in from the beginning. Here are some actions to consider:

- Define the roles that need to be involved across the AI lifecycle—not just at launch.

- Map the critical interaction points between functions and design rituals to support them (like shared sprint demos or pre-launch alignment meetings).

- Document a shared vocabulary, especially for ethically or legally sensitive terms like "bias," "consent," or "explainability."

- Use team formats that suit your maturity. If you're just starting, task forces might be enough. As you grow, enabling teams becomes key.

- Don't forget about adaptation. Your collaboration model should be flexible enough to evolve in response to regulatory changes, new tooling, or internal learnings.

Cross-functional collaboration isn't a warm and fuzzy ideal. It's a risk mitigation strategy. It's a productivity booster. And most importantly, it's how we make sure AI systems don't just work technically, but work for the people they're meant to serve.

MLOps as a balance for strategic planning

MLOps might sound like the opposite of strategy. After all, "ops" is about execution, and strategy is about direction. But when it comes to enterprise AI, the two are deeply intertwined. You can't scale what you can't operationalize. And no strategy is truly effective until it is reflected in how things are built, deployed, and maintained.

MLOps has been around for a while, and for good reason. It brings structure, discipline, and traceability to machine learning workflows. However, what is often overlooked is that it also serves as a bridge between humans and machines. MLOps creates the space where automation and human oversight coexist—where models can learn and evolve, but not in a black box.

The core practices of MLOps[28] typically include:

- **Versioning**: Tracking model changes over time, including datasets, parameters, and code.

- **Reproducibility**: Ensuring others (or future you) can replicate results under the same conditions.

- **Continuous Integration / Continuous Deployment (CI/CD)**: Automating testing and rollout pipelines.

- **Monitoring**: Keeping tabs on model drift, data quality, and performance in production.

- **Retraining**: Updating models when performance degrades or the world changes.

This sounds technical—and it is—but its implications are organizational. MLOps doesn't live in a vacuum. It requires collaboration across data scientists, ML engineers, product managers, domain experts, and often legal or compliance teams. In fact, it's one of the few functions that inherently forces cross-functional interaction. And that makes it a powerful touchpoint for turning AI strategy into operational reality.

---

[28]Treveil, M., Omont, N., Stenac, C., Lefevre, K., Phan, D., Zentici, J., Lavoillotte, A., Miya zaki, M., Heidmann, L. (2020). Introducing MLOps. O'Reilly Media.

Take this fictional (but familiar) example. *Imagine you're at a financial services company rolling out an AI-powered risk scoring tool. The strategy team defined a clear objective: improve customer onboarding speed while maintaining compliance. The ML engineers build a model, but without MLOps practices, they struggle with inconsistent test results, manual deployments, and unclear retraining triggers. Meanwhile, the compliance team is nervous because they have no visibility into how often the model changes or why.*

Now introduce MLOps. Suddenly, there's a shared language—versioning logs for the auditors, dashboards for product leads, and alerts for the engineers. Retraining happens based on defined thresholds. Everyone's working from the same playbook, even if they're on different teams. That's not just better operations—that's strategy in action.

In short, MLOps turns ideas into impact. If your AI strategy aspires to scale, sustain, and evolve, then it needs to meet MLOps somewhere in the middle. Because this isn't just about deployment, it's about responsibility, repeatability, and respect for the humans who rely on these systems.

Follow the pain

If you've ever tried launching an AI use case in a big organization, you know the temptation. Build something dazzling. Start with a moonshot. Show what's possible and win hearts with a big bang. The problem? That thinking often leads straight to what I lovingly call "pilot theater"—impressive prototypes that generate buzz but quietly fizzle out because they didn't solve a real problem for anyone.

Follow the pain.

Not the trend, not the hype, not the tech. The pain. Where are people in your organization frustrated? Where are they spending hours on tasks that add little value? Where are customers complaining, where are employees creating their own inefficient workarounds, and where is the business losing time or money? These aren't just symptoms of inefficiency—they're invitations. Signals. And if we're smart, we treat them as the starting point for meaningful AI applications. Because pain points, by their nature, rarely belong to a single team. They cut across departments, expose broken handoffs, and surface the messy reality of how work gets done. Which means solving them doesn't just require AI—it requires collaboration.

And that's the beautiful twist. Following the pain becomes an inherently collaborative act. When you start with a real, cross-functional problem, you also create a shared interest in the solution. You're not asking people to align around abstract outcomes. You're helping them rally around something tangible—something that already hurts. The people who feel the pain, the people who can fix it, and the people who benefit from it are suddenly in the same room. And when that happens, you're no longer pushing an AI agenda. You're co-creating value, and that value turns into advocacy that attracts information about more pain points.

Take this fictional example. *A logistics company is struggling with a flood of customer support tickets related to delivery delays. Meanwhile, the AI strategy team is focused on developing a predictive model for demand forecasting. Impressive? Sure. But not urgent. Customer service agents feel the real pain of manually triaging delay complaints, operations managers juggle last-minute rerouting, and IT tries to keep their homegrown systems patched together. So the AI team pivots. They collaborate with support and operations to develop a model that predicts delay reasons and recommends personalized customer responses in real-time. What happens next isn't magic—it's trust. Customer support sees relief. Ops gets better foresight. The AI team earns credibility. And suddenly, the effort is no longer isolated. It's owned.*

This is precisely the kind of use case where collaboration feels natural, not forced. Where AI doesn't feel like something imposed from above, but something developed with and for the people who need it. And when you solve real problems effectively, you want to make sure they stay solved—which is exactly why the operational excellence we discussed with MLOps becomes critical. But the foundation is always the same: start where it hurts.

The real point is this: solving real problems builds real relationships. When someone sees their pain being addressed, not with a theoretical roadmap but with an actual working solution, they're more likely to become a supporter. Maybe even a champion. That kind of emotional investment is worth more than a dozen innovation workshops. It's how you build bottom-up momentum that sustains AI transformation when budgets fluctuate or leadership changes. And it works especially well when teams have been burned before by flashy tech that never delivered.

> *Pain isn't just a signal of inefficiency. It's a test of intent. If you ignore it, people notice. If you solve it, people remember. And they talk. They tell others. That's how word-of-mouth spreads inside organizations—not from newsletters or townhalls, but from people saying: "Hey, this AI thing actually helped me."*

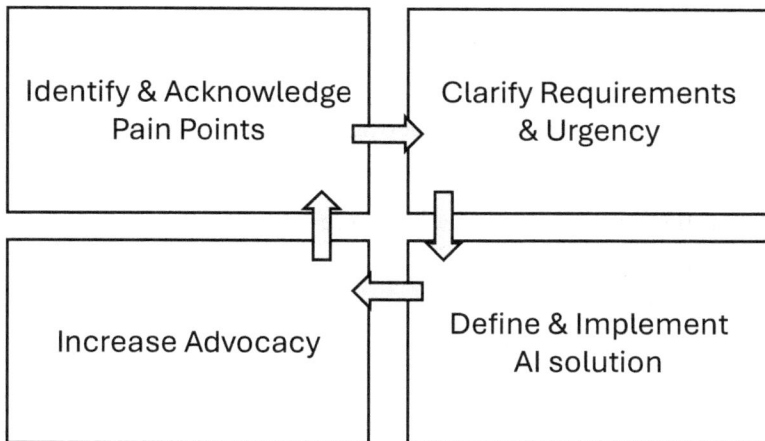

Figure 5: "Follow the pain" cycle.

It's also how you scale without scaling prematurely. When you follow the pain in one team, you often uncover broader patterns.

Suddenly, that delay prediction model has use cases in other regions—the architecture scales. The model generalizes—the trust compounds. And now you have something far more potent than a pilot—you have a platform for ongoing collaboration.

So yes, have vision. Think big. Talk about transformation. But when it comes to where you start, follow the pain. Let that guide your collaborations, your priorities, and your investments. Because every solved pain point is not just a win—it's an open door to build better, together.

The power of communities

When organizations discuss their AI strategy, the default approach is often top-down: roadmaps, executive sponsors, budgets, and centralized steering committees. However, the reality is that the energy sustaining an AI strategy usually comes from the bottom up. That's where communities come in— informal, self-organized, often messy but surprisingly powerful.

Communities of practice, prompt libraries, internal guilds, knowledge-sharing forums—these aren't just nice-to-haves. They're where the real learning happens. They create the space for people to experiment, fail safely, exchange ideas, and build shared vocabulary. In a space as volatile and fast-moving as AI, no single team or leader can keep up with everything. Communities are how knowledge gets distributed, refined, and normalized across functions and hierarchies.

One of the reasons communities work so well is that they're resilient to organizational change. Restructures, reorgs, new operating models—these things tend to hit formal teams hard. But communities? They're usually hierarchy-agnostic. They operate on the basis of mutual interest, trust, and shared curiosity. That makes them incredibly durable, even when everything else is shifting.

Of course, not all AI communities are the same. Some are deeply technical, such as groups of RAG enthusiasts exchanging notes on integrating retrieval-augmented generation into their product stack. Others are more focused on craft, like prompting guilds that build and test effective prompts for GenAI tools. Then there are ethics circles, where people debate the dilemmas AI brings into their daily work, and applied AI meetups that bring together designers, developers, and business leads to share prototypes and real-world stories.

What's interesting is that AI can also help drive these communities. From suggesting content based on shared interests to summarizing discussion threads to intelligently matching learning partners, generative AI can make community learning more accessible and scalable. That's a powerful feedback loop: communities shaping AI use, and AI shaping how communities grow.

If you're shaping an AI strategy in your organization, don't just encourage communities—legitimize them. Make space for them to thrive. Provide infrastructure, sure, but also acknowledge the invisible work that goes into sustaining them. When someone leads a prompt guild or runs a biweekly AI brown bag, they're not just being nice—they're doing strategic work. Recognize it. Include it in performance reviews (if they're willing). Give them "community time" in their calendars. Because in the end, the bridges they build across silos might be the most critical infrastructure your AI strategy has.

Collaboration in data-rich, label-hungry AI projects

When we discuss AI systems, especially those powered by machine learning, we often celebrate the algorithms and overlook the fundamental truth: no model learns without examples. Supervised learning, the cornerstone of many traditional and generative AI applications, thrives on labeled data. And while many organizations have vast reservoirs of raw data, what they often lack is the labeled kind—the curated, annotated, judgment-applied data that makes AI useful.

Labeling isn't just a mechanical task. It's an act of translation—transforming human context into machine-readable signals. That's why it requires deep collaboration between different groups: domain experts who understand the data's meaning, annotators who can apply consistent and accurate labels, and data scientists who transform these labels into models. Without this collaborative triangle, errors multiply, bias creeps in, and AI performance suffers.

And here's the kicker: this problem gets even more complex in the world of unstructured data. In generative AI use cases, we're not just labeling whether a transaction was fraudulent or not. We're assessing whether a chatbot's answer was correct, whether the tone was appropriate, and whether the source was recent and reliable. These are judgments only humans can make—and they're not easy.

The need for labeled data is growing, not shrinking.

Examples are everywhere. HR teams need labeled transcripts of conversations to train recruiting bots. Legal teams must review and annotate contracts to assist large language models in generating accurate summaries. Customer support logs are reviewed for emotional tone, hallucinations, or risky advice. This is no longer a niche technical concern—it has become an enterprise-wide responsibility.

And yet, many still treat data labeling as an outsourced, invisible backend task. But you can't outsource accountability. Especially when models are trained on sensitive or high-stakes data, the organization must retain oversight and domain expertise. This isn't just about accuracy—it's about ethics, compliance, and trust.

That's why AI strategy must explicitly plan for human-in-the-loop (as previously mentioned in the Competence chapter) data labeling, not as an afterthought, but as a core function. It means building governance for label quality and ownership. It means training internal subject matter experts and annotators. It means investing in user-friendly tools that make labeling efficient, intuitive, and scalable. And most of all, it means aligning these labeling efforts with high-impact AI use cases, so teams know that their work directly connects to value creation.

If AI is only as good as the data it learns from—and that data depends on human judgment—then the work of labeling must be seen for what it truly is: a form of collaboration. One that deserves recognition, resources, and a prominent seat at the AI strategy table.

Trust is not optional

Trust has always been the invisible glue that holds collaboration together. We feel it when it's present, and we notice its absence immediately, especially when things go wrong. With AI entering the room—sometimes loudly, sometimes subtly—our trust dynamics are becoming increasingly complex.

Trust in AI doesn't just mean trusting the tool. It means trusting the people who created it, the teams who govern it, and the processes in which it's embedded. It also means trusting that the

AI is being used *for* us, not *against* us. And as much as we'd like to believe in the inherent neutrality of algorithms, we know better: trust has to be earned, not assumed.

The challenge is that AI often shows up in ways that are invisible or asymmetrical. One person on a team might fully understand when AI is in play and how it works. Others might be unaware, or even misled, especially if the interface makes the AI feel "human." This gap can create confusion, suspicion, or even resentment. It's hard to collaborate when one half of the team doesn't know a machine is part of it.

That's why one of the most foundational elements of AI collaboration is **disclosure**. People deserve to know when they're interacting with or being evaluated by a system that's partially or fully AI-driven. Whether it's a chatbot answering a question, a model flagging a customer for review, or a tool suggesting performance feedback, transparency is essential. Small signals, such as icons, watermarks, or "AI assistant" tags, can go a long way. So, regular check-ins can occur where teams discuss what's working, what feels off, and how the AI is evolving.

> *Trust doesn't just happen between humans and AI.*
> *It occurs between humans due to AI.*

If a model decides on a team workflow, and no one knows how it got there, fingers start pointing. If one department automates something and another doesn't understand the implications, silos deepen. It's not just a technical problem—it's a communication one.

To build trust, we need more than model cards or ethics principles pinned to the wall. We need **feedback loops** that work in both directions: humans evaluating AI outputs, yes, but also systems that learn from human context and corrections. We need psychological safety, so people feel secure in admitting they don't understand an AI recommendation or disagree with it. We also need intentional practices in teams to normalize discussing AI, just as we would any other team member, without assuming it has feelings.

That also means being honest about the limits. AI isn't a magical teammate. It doesn't share accountability. It doesn't take responsibility when things go wrong. And it certainly doesn't build trust on its own. That's still our job.

Here's what to do: take time to make trust explicit. Don't just ask "Does the AI work?" Ask, "Do we *trust* how it works, and *how it's used*?" Make it a habit to discuss AI use openly, regularly, and without shame, acknowledging that you may not know all the details.

Whether we're collaborating with AI, around AI, or despite AI, it's the quality of trust between humans that ultimately determines whether we succeed together.

And one of the most powerful ways to build that trust? Communication. That's where we're headed in the next chapter.

FIVE

Communication

Communication might seem like the soft side of AI strategy, but let's be real, it's often the hardest. It's not just about having good slide decks or clear documentation. It's about how people understand each other, how they interact with machines, and how machines respond back. In AI strategy, we're dealing with communication on three levels: human-to-human, human-to-AI, and AI-to-human. All three need to be designed with intention, not left to chance.

The truth is, many AI initiatives don't fail because of technical shortcomings. They fail due to misunderstandings of expectations, unclear responsibilities, and a lack of trust in what the system is actually doing. If we can't explain AI clearly, people won't adopt it—or worse, they'll misuse it.

Once AI systems begin communicating with humans—answering questions, writing content, even making decisions—they become part of the organization's voice. And if that voice feels confusing, robotic, or untrustworthy, users tune out. Internally, communication is the most powerful tool we have to address AI fatigue and anxiety. Not everyone needs to understand how the models work, but everyone deserves to know what they do, why they matter, and how they impact their work.

Externally, we also have to resist the urge to oversell. AI isn't magic—it's a tool. A powerful one, yes, but one that still needs human oversight and common sense. That means our narratives around AI need to be grounded, responsible, and accessible.

Throughout this chapter, we'll examine how to align expectations, communicate AI's purpose and limitations, humanize its outputs, and embed communication as an integral part of any AI strategy, rather than an afterthought.

Finding your AI purpose

Before we dive into how to communicate about AI, let's take a step back and ask a deeper question:

Why are you using AI in the first place?

That might sound philosophical, but it's actually a very practical question, because if you can't clearly articulate your AI purpose, it's going to be very difficult to explain it to anyone else.

Like the data purpose I outlined in my previous book, the AI purpose sits at the intersection of four things: what is exciting to do, what aligns with business strategy, what is ethical to do, and what is feasible to do. It's not just a sweet spot—it's a strategic compass that keeps everyone aligned when the AI hype gets overwhelming. And finding that intersection isn't just an internal reflection. It's a conversation. Because before a purpose can be communicated, it needs to be co-created. That means the different voices of technical, business, ethical, and operational parties need to be part of the discussion. If they've helped shape the purpose, they're much more likely to carry it forward with clarity and conviction.

Figure 6: AI Purpose Framework.

Let's break down what these four elements mean:

- **What is exciting to do**: This is about energy and inspiration. What would people in your organization love to see AI do? What kinds of impact motivate action?

- **What is aligned with business strategy**: Your AI efforts should reinforce your broader business goals, not distract from them or float in isolation.

- **What is ethical to do**: Just because something is possible doesn't mean it should be done. Ethical boundaries give your strategy integrity and sustainability.

- **What is feasible to do**: Practicality matters. You need the data, the skills, and the infrastructure actually to make it happen.

A meaningful AI purpose helps set guardrails. It helps you decide which use cases to prioritize, which technologies to invest in, and which trade-offs are acceptable. If the only thing guiding your AI program is "Let's automate more" or "Let's use AI to be more efficient," you're missing the point. That kind of vague ambition doesn't inspire anyone, and it doesn't help your teams make aligned decisions. The best AI purposes are concrete enough to guide choices, broad enough to evolve, and grounded enough to earn trust.

This clarity also helps you say no to the wrong things, such as hype-driven experiments that don't align with your goals or values. It helps reduce the scattershot effect, where different teams pursue disconnected pilots with no coherence. And perhaps most importantly, it provides your organization with a language to discuss AI that is grounded in meaning, not just mechanics.

But your AI purpose isn't something you set once and forget. Just like business strategy, it needs to evolve. As your organization evolves, as your people become more proficient in AI capabilities, and as new technologies emerge, your purpose may shift. That's not a problem—it's a sign of maturity. The key is to revisit it often enough so that it stays relevant, and to keep communicating it so that everyone can pull in the same direction.

> *Before you worry about perfecting your AI messaging, get your purpose straight.*

If you can't answer why you're using AI in a way that excites and aligns your people, then no amount of communication polish will make your strategy land.

Framing AI's value for different audiences

If you want people to support your AI strategy, they need to understand what's in it for them, not just what's in it for the "business" (because who is the "business" anyway?). That means framing the value of AI on both an organizational and an individual level. And the key word here is "framing," not just "explaining." Because how you talk about AI's value is as essential as the value itself.

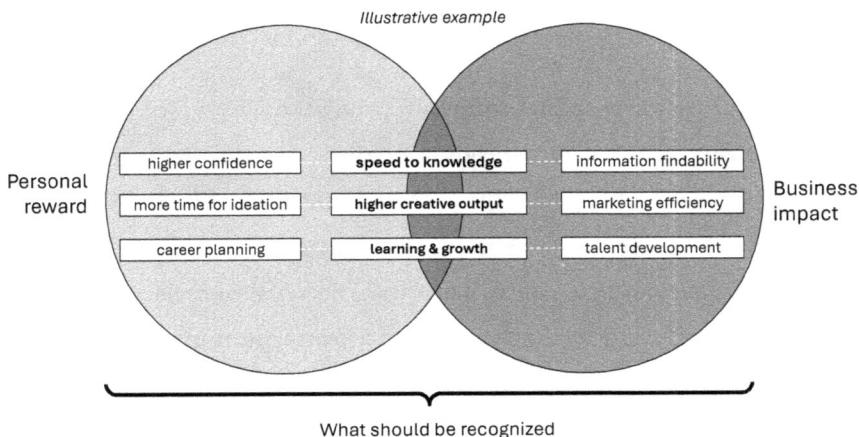

Figure 7: Value framing

Take, for example, an AI-powered knowledge assistant rolled out across a consulting firm. At the organizational level, the value is speed and scale—consultants can find relevant templates, client references, or case studies in seconds, which improves client delivery and increases utilization. But at the individual level, the value is personal—a junior consultant no longer feels lost in SharePoint folders, and a manager saves hours per week preparing for client workshops.

Or imagine a generative AI content tool introduced in the marketing department. The company frames it as a way to generate more campaign material without hiring additional staff, but that's unlikely to resonate unless you also address its implications for the team. For a copywriter, the real value might be getting through first drafts faster, freeing up time for creative ideation. For a marketing analyst, this might involve using AI to summarize social media comments and identify emerging customer themes.

And in HR, let's say you introduce an AI model that supports internal mobility by recommending personalized learning paths. Organizationally, that supports talent development and retention goals. But individually, it helps employees understand how they can grow—and where they might go next in their careers. That's a very different kind of value proposition, and one that needs to be communicated just as clearly.

If you ignore the individual perspective and focus solely on company-wide benefits, you risk sounding abstract or even threatening. On the other hand, if you only talk about personal productivity gains without linking them to strategy, it can feel like a gimmick.

The best framing connects the dots between business outcomes and human experiences.

It also needs to address fear, especially around job loss or relevance. Don't just say, "AI won't take your job." That rings hollow. Say instead: "We're using AI to reduce repetitive work so you can focus on the parts of your job that require judgment, creativity, or empathy." Then back it up with real examples and visible changes.

Avoid vague, sweeping statements like "AI will transform everything." That might be technically true, but it's emotionally unhelpful. Focus instead on concrete use cases and the specific types of value they bring. Different stakeholders care about different things. Executives want to see how AI drives strategy. Mid-level managers want to know what changes they need to lead. Frontline employees want to feel supported, not blindsided.

Your framing should also include both the "why now" and the "why us." Why is this the right time to introduce AI in your organization? And why is your team the right one to drive it? These questions often go unspoken, but they shape people's trust more than any technical proof point.

And remember, good framing is not a one-time presentation. It's a continuous conversation that evolves with your AI journey. As use cases mature and capabilities grow, so too should the narrative around their value. What people need to hear on day one will be different from what they need to hear six months in.

The better you get at telling this story in the language that resonates with your audience, the stronger your AI strategy will become because a strategy that can't be communicated is a strategy that won't be followed.

Managing AI stakeholder personas

One of the biggest mistakes in AI strategy is assuming that everyone sees it the same way. Spoiler alert: they don't. Some people see AI as the next big leap. Others see it as a risk. Some are cautiously curious, and some would rather not deal with it at all. And you know what? That's completely normal. We're not managing robots here (even if some people act like they are). We're managing humans with different experiences, values, fears, and levels of understanding.

That's why part of any human-centric AI strategy is understanding the types of people you're communicating with. Not in a reductive way, but as a way to navigate the complexity of change. Think of it like stakeholder mapping, but through the lens of attitudes toward AI. For example, I've experienced these four different personas:

- **The Visionary**: Someone excited about AI's transformative potential. They want to go fast and big. They're great allies for momentum, but they may need some grounding in ethical or practical limits.

- **The Cautious Pragmatist**: Curious but careful. They want to see results, proof of value, and risk mitigation before committing. Win them over with ROI and small, low-risk wins.

- **The Skeptic**: Often the hardest to engage. They may not believe AI has real benefits, or they may have been burned by past hype. With them, it's about building trust and offering transparency.

- **The Ethical Guardian**: Focused on fairness, safety, and unintended consequences. They're not against AI, but they want to ensure it's developed responsibly. Their concerns are often vital, and they deserve real answers, not PR statements.

Most of us don't fit neatly into just one of these categories—we shift depending on context, past experiences, or what's at stake. Someone might be visionary in one project and deeply skeptical in another. The point is to tailor your communication. Not everyone responds to tech specs or cost savings. Some want guardrails. Some want inspiration. Some want a way to opt out.

When you're operationalizing an AI strategy, you don't get to choose who's in the room.

You must work with visionaries and skeptics, pragmatists and guardians. So the communication needs to work for all of them. If it only resonates with the people already on board, it's not really a strategy—it's a silo.

Creating something like an AI persona map can be a useful tool. Not to label people, but to anticipate where alignment will be easy and where it needs more intentional effort. It's a simple reminder that AI isn't just a technical system. It's a social one too. And social systems are complex, messy, and full of emotion. That's why our words, stories, and tone matter just as much as our frameworks and roadmaps.

So if you're building an AI strategy, don't just ask, "What do we need to say?" Ask, "Who are we saying it to and what will they hear?" That's where the real work begins.

Making AI-driven work visible and valuable

AI-generated outputs often look polished, insightful, and effortless—but that polish can hide a messy and invisible trail of human effort. A chatbot that instantly gives a helpful answer didn't happen by magic. It's the result of weeks or months of iterative development, guardrail testing, and alignment discussions. A beautiful dashboard forecasting next month's revenue? Behind it might be years of historical data cleaning, context setting, and wrangling from across half a dozen business units. The slickness of the surface makes it easy to forget the complexity beneath it. The same invisibility problem exists with traditional AI—that fraud detection model blocking transactions has months of feature engineering behind it, but customers only see payment declined.

This is where the communication challenge starts. If we only show the output, we create unrealistic expectations about how AI works—and worse, what it takes to make it work. That's why part of humanizing AI strategy is making the invisible visible. It's not about venting or playing defense. It's about giving a real sense of effort versus outcome—a kind of internal ROI mindset. When people understand what goes into delivering an AI-enabled capability, they're more likely to use it responsibly, appreciate its limits, and think twice before demanding an AI "solution" where a simple Excel sheet would do.

There's also an element of empathy. Once people realize that AI features don't just appear—that behind every model is a team of designers, data professionals, engineers, testers, reviewers—it creates space for better collaboration. People become more mindful of what they're requesting. It's no longer "Let's plug in AI", but rather "Do we really need AI for this, and what would it take?" That's a win for both efficiency and morale.

The same principle applies when an AI application goes live. Don't just show the shiny demo or business case headline. Tell the story. What were the hard parts? What surprised the team? What trade-offs had to be made? Sharing the journey—not just the destination—helps normalize the effort behind innovation. It also builds psychological safety for future projects. When others see that even successful AI initiatives have setbacks, they're more likely to start experimenting themselves.

This kind of transparency builds trust. Most people don't fear AI because they dislike the concept—they fear the unknown. That fear shrinks when they can see how AI is used, what guardrails are in place, and how it connects to real business logic. And no, this doesn't mean publishing model weights or diving into TensorFlow. It's about providing legibility through story maps, simplified diagrams, internal showcases, and even short behind-the-scenes videos. Make it understandable, not inscrutable.

Equally important is to connect AI outputs to actual value. Whether it's cost savings, improved service quality, reduced errors, or better customer experience, make the impact tangible. Technical success doesn't always equal business adoption. But perceived usefulness? That's what drives uptake. And that perception is shaped by how well we communicate the story behind the solution.

Lastly, don't forget to celebrate the humans. When a team builds something meaningful with AI, share it. Shine a light not just on the model, but on the mindset, effort, and creativity that went into it. It reinforces shared ownership. It nurtures learning. And it reminds us all that even in an AI-driven world, the people still matter most.

Shared semantical context is key

We've just talked about making AI work visible and valuable. But there's a hidden challenge: AI systems often fail not because they're technically broken, but because they don't understand what we mean. Ask three departments to define "customer" and you'll get four different answers. One says it's anyone who's ever bought something. Another insists it's only active subscribers. A third includes free trial users. This isn't just semantic nitpicking—it's the difference between AI that actually helps and AI that confidently gives you the wrong answer.

This is where the so-called semantic layer comes in. Think of it as a shared dictionary that helps AI understand your business the way you do. It's the translation layer between how your organization communicates and how data systems store information. In its most powerful form, this becomes a knowledge graph—a network that maps not just definitions but relationships. It knows that customers place orders, orders contain products, and products have suppliers. It's not just a dictionary—it's your organization's mental map.

Without it, you get technically correct but practically useless results. For instance, when the sales AI reports "zero customer churn" because it's only looking at enterprise accounts, while your actual problem is that small businesses are leaving too quickly. The AI isn't wrong—it just doesn't know what you meant by "customer."

Building this shared understanding requires bringing people from different departments together to agree on the meaning of specific words. What counts as a "lead"? When does a "project" officially start? What's the difference between "revenue" and "recognized revenue"? These conversations can be painful because they surface all the hidden assumptions and conflicting definitions that have been causing friction for years. But that pain is productive. Once you align on meaning, you can encode it into systems that AI can understand and use consistently.

The payoff is huge. When AI knows that "high-value customer" means the same thing to sales, support, and finance, it can help coordinate across departments. When it understands that "urgent" in operations means something different from "urgent" in marketing, it can prioritize appropriately. Knowledge graphs turn these definitions into connected intelligence. When your AI understands not only what a "high-value customer" is, but also how they relate to purchase patterns, support tickets, and referral networks, it can surface insights that humans might miss.

This isn't about constraining language—
it's about giving AI a map of your business reality.

I could spend pages walking you through specific examples of semantic layers—showing you data models, ontologies, or how knowledge graphs connect "customer" to "orders" to "products." But that would turn this into a technical manual, and that's not what this book is about. What matters for our human-centric AI strategy is understanding that this translation layer exists, why it's critical for making AI actually useful, and that building it is fundamentally about human agreement, not technical architecture.

If you want to dive deeper into the practical implementation, I recommend two excellent resources: *Semantic Modeling for Data:*

Avoiding Pitfalls and Breaking Dilemmas by Panos Alexopoulos (O'Reilly Media, 2020), and *Designing and Building Enterprise Knowledge Graphs* by Juan Sequeda and Ora Lassila (Springer International Publishing, 2022). Both books will provide the technical depth that I'm deliberately skipping here.

Transparency leads to trust

When people hear "transparency in AI," most assume it means open algorithms or accessible documentation. But for AI strategy, that's not nearly enough. In previous chapters, we already established that trust is foundational to any human-AI interaction and that transparency plays a central role in building it. What we'll focus on here is how transparency *actually needs to be implemented and communicated* to make that trust real and sustainable.

First, let's address the gap between technical explainability and user-facing clarity. AI developers might understand confidence intervals, latent weights, or the architecture of a transformer—but that doesn't help your customer success agent understand why the chatbot responded in a strange tone, or why a forecast model suddenly got worse. If transparency lives only in the dev team's documentation, it doesn't serve its purpose.

Instead, we need to treat transparency as a communication and UX challenge. We have to design transparency touchpoints into the experience of using AI, things like:

- Plain-language summaries of what an AI system does and doesn't do.

- Confidence scores that are visible and interpretable by non-technical users.

- Side-by-side examples showing model behavior in different scenarios.

- Clear escalation paths when something seems off.

And yes, that includes the infrastructure surrounding the model as well. Metadata repositories and AI marketplaces can consist of key facts: What data was used for training? What version is running? What are the known limitations? These are the kinds of artifacts that help users form the right expectations and help organizations prove accountability when needed.

Explainability and interpretability are not just technical tasks. They are design and storytelling tasks. They require collaboration between engineers, designers, product owners, and yes, communicators. Your internal knowledge base should explain model intent in the same tone you'd use to brief your CEO or train a new hire.

> *Ultimately, AI systems don't just need to be right—*
> *they need to be understood.*

A powerful description of this challenge comes from *Atlas of AI* by Kate Crawford (Yale University Press, 2021), which explores how AI systems embed layers of decision-making and assumptions, many of which are invisible to end users. Crawford's work reminds us that what's hidden is often just as impactful as what's shown, and that transparency isn't a luxury—it's a safeguard against misuse, confusion, and distrust.

> *Make transparency operational.*

Define what explainability looks like for your users, not just your developers. Build interpretability into the experience, not just the backend. And when you think about trust, don't just assume it— earn it, one clear explanation at a time.

Designing AI conversations inside and out

When we think about conversations in an AI-enabled organization, it's no longer just human-to-human. It's human to AI, AI to human, and sometimes even AI to AI before it comes back to a person. That's a lot of conversational complexity to manage. And while many AI systems use natural language as their interface, that doesn't mean they automatically know how to communicate effectively, respectfully, or clearly. We still have to design those conversations with intention.

Whether we're talking about a customer-facing chatbot, an internal knowledge assistant, or a GenAI-powered productivity copilot, the same rule applies: communication needs to be clear, contextual, and aligned with the tone of your organization. That tone might differ depending on the tool and audience—a finance assistant should probably sound more formal than a creative brainstorming bot—but there should be consistency in how the AI represents your values. This is not just a brand exercise, it's a trust-building one.

That also means signaling clearly when a user is speaking to an AI system. People deserve to know whether they're talking to a machine, what kind of machine it is, and what the boundaries are. If the AI can't help, what happens next? Is there a handover to a human? Is there a defined escalation process? These questions need answers, not just technically, but in the flow of the conversation. Effective AI conversation design incorporates escalation logic and accommodates ambiguity, allowing for human fallbacks.

It's worth remembering that tone and intent are fragile things. Even between two people, misunderstandings often occur, especially when there are cultural, language, or accessibility differences. When we ask AI to communicate with us, it's crucial to involve cross-functional teams in defining how those conversations occur. UX writers, legal teams, designers, behavioral scientists, and domain experts—they all have a role to play. The conversation doesn't just happen in the UI, it lives in the architecture of the system, the prompt templates, and the response logic.

And then there's the funny reality of how much our communication norms are already shifting. With AI tools becoming such a big part of daily workflows, I wouldn't be surprised if some of us start speaking in prompts during meetings. I've caught myself doing it—barking out a question in "prompt mode" to a teammate instead of phrasing it like a human request. Spoiler: it didn't go over well. Just because AI understands us that way doesn't mean our colleagues appreciate it.

The best way for AI to learn how to communicate well is still the oldest one in the book: human examples. Lots of them. Fresh ones. The risk of overusing AI-generated content to train future AI systems—a process now being referred to as "recursive AI training"—is that we begin training machines on the output of other machines. That degrades tone, clarity, and nuance over time, like a game of telephone with no human at the start.

So, what should this mean for your AI strategy? First, conversational design deserves dedicated effort. If you want your AI to reflect your brand, team, or values, you must incorporate this aspect into your implementation plan. That includes investing in tone-of-voice libraries, prompt repositories, and escalation workflows. It means creating labeling standards so users know what's machine-generated. And it means maintaining a rhythm of regular reviews, because communication evolves—and so should your AI.

AI strategy documents should explicitly reflect these priorities. They should point to artifacts like conversational guidelines, prompt templates, escalation protocols, and cross-functional review cadences. Because communication is not just a surface-level experience—it's where understanding is built or broken. And in an AI-powered world, getting that right is one of the most human things we can do.

Guardrails, not uniformity

Have you ever noticed how, when AI writes everything, every single email or social media post starts sounding suspiciously alike? Or when did using em dashes become the primary indicator of AI-generated text? It's like walking into a party where everyone's wearing the exact same outfit—not exactly memorable (and probably a bit creepy).

The problem isn't AI itself—it's treating consistency like it's identical twins with uniformity. Yes, your brand needs to be recognizable. But recognizable doesn't mean cloning every word, phrase, or punctuation mark.

Here's what to do instead: set flexible guardrails, not rigid rails. Start with your core brand values. If your brand's voice is "optimistic but never cheesy" or "direct but always respectful", guide AI prompts toward those principles, not toward the exact same corporate-approved wording. Context matters—a lot. Let your people dial up the formality when emailing your board and dial it down when responding to customers on Twitter.

One-size-fits-all rarely fits anyone well, except maybe in ponchos—and even then, it's debatable.

Also, celebrate linguistic diversity. Let your team in Berlin use expressions that resonate locally, and allow your colleagues in Tokyo to weave in cultural nuance. People aren't just human—they're wonderfully different humans, and that's something to embrace, not flatten out.

Your AI tools should also know when to say "I'm not sure." Acting completely certain about unclear details might sound confident, but it often goes terribly wrong, like walking straight into a glass door. Keep your AI real and relatable—phrases like "possibly" or "it seems" aren't weaknesses, they're honesty.

What could these flexible guardrails look like in practice? Imagine having a "voice matrix" with sliders for warmth, playfulness, formality, and detail—your content creators can slide these around within certain safe ranges to match the context. Provide prompt recipes that include placeholders for tone adjustments, nudging authors to add their personal spice while staying in the flavor profile of your brand. Review tools could gently point out when something sounds way off, instead of nitpicking every sentence. And try tracking a "Voice Variety Score"—counting how many different words and phrases you use to make sure you're not starting to sound like a robot.

To keep these guardrails current without causing bureaucratic nightmares, create a lean "Voice Steward Circle"—a diverse group from UX, branding, legal, DEI, and support that meets regularly to recalibrate guidelines as markets, regulations, or cultures shift. Use automated checks for low-risk messages and brief, human "tone sweeps" for major external communications. Efficient, agile, and human-centric governance is achievable if approached thoughtfully.

Remember from the previous section, we talked about the importance of regularly feeding fresh, human-created examples into your AI's training loop. Recursive self-training might sound efficient, but without fresh human content, it quickly devolves into a weird game of AI "telephone," diluting authenticity with every round. Also, regularly check how your audience perceives the tone of your content and incorporate their feedback on a quarterly basis.

Ultimately, success looks like external readers confidently recognizing your brand voice without sensing a monotonous algorithm behind it. Internally, your employees should feel empowered to express their authentic selves within clear yet flexible brand boundaries.

Clearly define your brand's "safe corridor" for voice and establish your "Voice Steward Circle."

Pilot your flexible toolkit on a single visible external channel, closely monitor your "Voice Variety Score," and iteratively adjust your guardrails. It's time to ensure your brand's human voice not only survives but thrives.

With clear yet flexible guardrails in place, your teams won't just preserve their authentic voice—they'll be empowered to experiment creatively. And that creative empowerment is precisely what we need to explore next.

While maintaining voice consistency is important, it's just one part of a larger question: How do we keep human creativity alive in an age of AI? How do we ensure that, as machines get better at generating content, humans don't lose their creative edge? That's where we're heading in the next chapter—into the heart of what makes us uniquely creative, and how AI can amplify rather than replace that human spark.

Six

Creativity

In an age where AI can write jingles, generate logos, and even finish your half-written poem, it's tempting to think creativity is becoming machine territory. But there's a big difference between remixing what already exists and inventing something that's never been seen before. AI is incredibly good at *incremental* creativity—polishing drafts, proposing variations, and combining styles. Human beings, though? We're the ones who create from zero. We invent new art forms, new worldviews, and yes, literal wheels. That kind of disruptive leap is still a profoundly human superpower.

Rather than replacing imagination, AI should be seen as an amplifier for it. The best creative setups today aren't man or machine—they're partnerships. It's a bit like having an endlessly patient, creative assistant who never sleeps and doesn't take your "weird idea" personally.

Of course, there are still a few myths to clear up. AI doesn't daydream, doodle, or get inspired. It predicts. It assembles. It imitates. That's not a bad thing—it just means we shouldn't pretend it's something it's not. Real creativity still needs the human layer of emotion, intention, and context. That's where the soul lives.

This chapter explores how to make the most of this new creative partnership. We'll start by focusing on generative AI—the headline-grabbing technology that's reshaping how we think about content creation, ideation, and creative workflows. But creativity isn't just about generating text and images. In the second half of this chapter, we'll explore how traditional AI—the predictive models, optimization algorithms, and pattern-recognition systems—also demands and enables human creativity in different but equally important ways. From frameworks that encourage playful ideation to examples of AI-fueled innovation that don't feel robotic, we'll explore how companies can tap into human imagination *with* AI instead of fighting against it. Ready to get a little weird and wonderfully original? Good, because this is where the real fun begins.

When humans disrupt and machines refine

Not all creativity is created equal. That might sound ironic in a chapter about AI, but it's a truth that gets overlooked way too often. When we talk about "creative AI," we're usually referring to systems that remix, generate, or synthesize based on existing inputs. That's impressive, no doubt, but it's not the same thing as human creativity. Humans can create from nothing. We make wild leaps. We imagine things that break every rule. Invent a new musical genre? Paint something no one's seen before? Change how people think? That's us. AI, on the other hand, excels at what I call *incremental creativity*—refining, tweaking, and spinning out twenty variations of a headline, or applying a known style to a new context.

This is where intent really matters. AI can simulate creativity, but it lacks purpose and intuition. It doesn't know why a particular image moves you, or why one version of a joke lands while another one falls flat. It lacks that uniquely human blend of context, emotion, tension, and contradiction—the friction that often fuels great ideas. For people, creating something is rarely a straight line. It's messy. It involves doubt, guts, and that weird gut-feeling we can't always explain. AI skips all that. It doesn't wrestle with creative blocks or stay up at night questioning the meaning of its output. It just…outputs.

Think of it as a spectrum. On the far left, we have *generative refinement*—AI's sweet spot. This is where speed, volume, and stylistic consistency shine. On the far right, we have *original disruption*—those truly human moments of groundbreaking innovation. And in the middle? That's *collaborative iteration*, where humans and AI work together to elevate ideas. It's the designer using AI to brainstorm layouts, then applying their own taste and storytelling instinct. It's the marketer testing different

AI-generated taglines, then rewriting the winner with just the right emotional punch. Different tasks sit at different points on this spectrum.

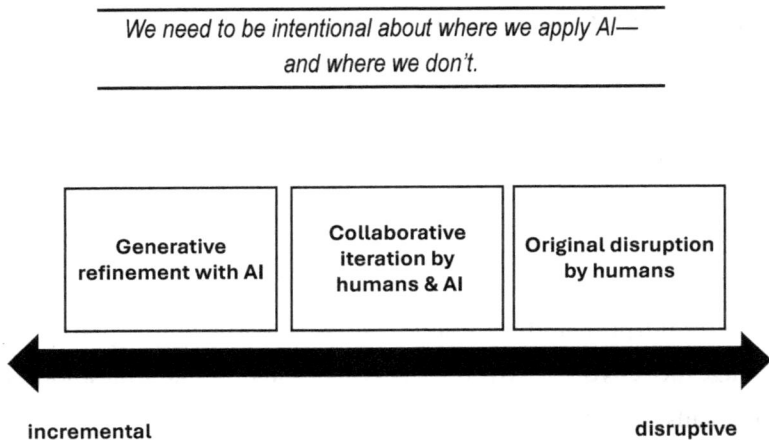

---

*We need to be intentional about where we apply AI—
and where we don't.*

Generative refinement with AI	Collaborative iteration by humans & AI	Original disruption by humans

incremental ←———————————————————→ **disruptive**

Figure 8: Creativity Spectrum.

Creativity isn't just about output. For humans, it's about experience. It's how we find meaning. It's how we connect with others, build identity, and feel proud of what we've made. When a machine "creates," it doesn't grow from the process—it just runs another cycle. So, from a strategy standpoint, leaders need to do more than assign creativity to the nearest generative model. They need to map their use cases to this spectrum, protect human space where it matters most, and design AI support systems that augment rather than overwrite human imagination. Let AI be the amplifier—but never the author of your creative soul.

The idea is the new execution

For years, creativity in business was mainly about *getting stuff done.* The big idea was important, sure—but the real challenge was executing it efficiently across a dozen channels, formats, and deadlines. Today, that part is increasingly handled by AI. Generating multiple layouts, running endless A/B tests, resizing images, drafting copy variations in a click—execution has never been faster or cheaper. What used to take teams days or weeks can now be done in minutes. This raises a larger question:

If AI handles the tasks, what are humans here for?

The answer is simple, yet transformative: we move upstream (or dare I say, "shift left"?). Instead of spending most of our time building assets, we start spending more time shaping ideas and framing the challenge. Asking better questions. Adding emotional depth and nuance. Crafting metaphors, sense-making, storytelling. These are the moments that define meaning, not just production. As AI speeds up output, ideation becomes the real bottleneck. That makes it the new premium skill. And it's not just "coming up with cool ideas." It's about creative prompting, reframing problems, curating inspiration from unexpected places, and imagining what doesn't yet exist.

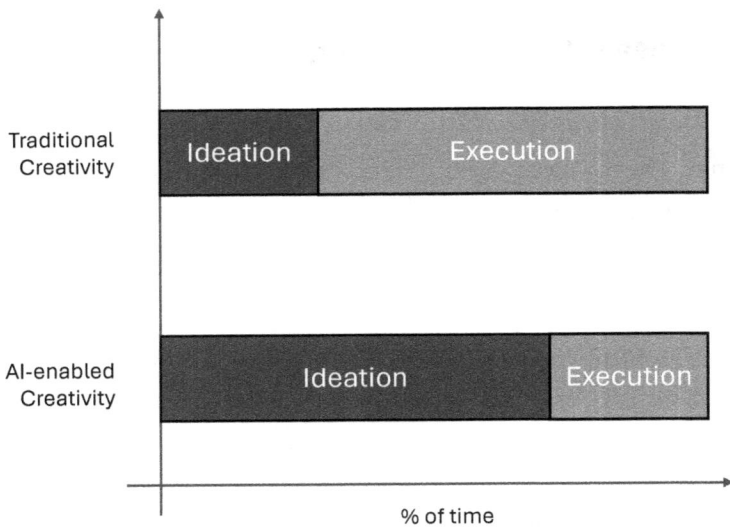

Figure 9: Value shift with AI-enabled creativity.

But faster execution comes with its own paradox. Just because you *can* do more doesn't mean you *should*. There's a risk of flooding the system with generic content, chasing quantity over quality. Human-centric creativity is about the slow burn—the pause, the iteration, the reflection that gives ideas texture and weight. It's about asking "Is this meaningful?" not just "Is this publishable?" That takes courage and intention in a world that constantly pushes for more.

To make the most of this shift, organizations must rethink how creative work is conducted. Start by giving people time to think bigger. Let teams question the brief itself, not just deliver what it asks for. Welcome messy exploration and "what if" thinking, even if it feels slower at first. Think of your brand voice like elastic—it should stretch and bend for different situations and people, without completely losing its shape. And most importantly, ensure that your AI strategy prioritizes human ideas.

Build tools, rewards, and workflows that support the dreamers and thinkers, not just the people checking boxes.

Prompting as a creative discipline

When most people hear the word *prompt*, they think of a quick instruction: "Write me a summary", "Generate ten ideas", "Make this sound smarter." But prompting, when done well, isn't about giving orders to a machine. It's about crafting direction. Prompting is an expressive, iterative, and increasingly essential component of any creative process involving AI. In many ways, the prompt has become the new creative brief.

A good prompt doesn't just describe what you want—it invites the model into your thought process. It sets a tone, offers context, and lays down useful constraints. Think of the difference between asking "Give me three campaign ideas" versus "Give me three campaign ideas that feel hopeful, sound like our brand, and could be used in both email and social." The first gets you quantity. The second one gets you aligned and purposeful output. That's not prompting as a hack—it's prompting as authorship.

And like any creative skill, it takes practice. Prompt fluency means knowing how to test, adjust, reframe, and iterate—not just to get better results, but to sharpen your thinking. It forces you to slow down and ask: What am I trying to say? What tone am I aiming for? What assumptions am I making? Prompting can even reveal your blind spots—what you've left unsaid, or what perspectives you've unconsciously prioritized. It's part technical, part strategic, part psychological mirror.

Most importantly, prompting is a way to embed values into the AI's outputs. If your organization values transparency, empathy, or curiosity, your prompts should reflect these values. And if you want a consistent voice, inclusive language, or cultural nuance, you can't just expect the model to "know"—you have to tell it. Build prompt libraries the same way you build communication guidelines. Let teams borrow from each other, remix what works, and develop a shared vocabulary. And give them time and space to play. Because prompting, like all creative work, isn't a formula—it's a craft. One that's worth treating with the same care we give to design, storytelling, and strategy.

Co-creating With AI

AI isn't just changing what we create—it's changing *who* creates, and *how*. Inside organizations, AI is becoming a powerful tool for internal co-creation. Instead of gathering a team in a room and hoping the best ideas survive the loudest voices, we can now bring

AI into the early stages of ideation. It becomes a silent, judgment-free collaborator that helps everyone—from the most outspoken to the most introverted—test thoughts, sketch alternatives, and remix ideas in real time or asynchronously. It's not replacing the whiteboard—it's about expanding it.

This new kind of collaboration means we need to think beyond just sharing outputs. Teams that embrace AI co-creation well don't just swap final drafts—they share *prompts*. "Here's what I asked, and here's what I got. Try tweaking it this way." It's a subtle shift, but it unlocks a whole new creative rhythm. Prompt libraries, shared templates, and even real-time co-prompting tools are turning AI from a personal productivity trick into a collaborative muscle. It's also more fun when you get to build weird and wonderful things together.

But co-creation doesn't stop at the company walls. AI is also enabling a new level of customer participation. From personalized product recommendations to build-your-own-experience interfaces, AI lets users shape content, services, and communication in ways that feel genuinely collaborative. Whether it's tuning the tone of a chatbot, customizing visuals in a report, or remixing a product bundle, customers are no longer just consuming—they're co-creating. And when done right, this kind of personalization feels less like marketing and more like mutual design.

That said, just because AI makes co-creation easy doesn't mean it's always appropriate. There are moments when co-creation with

AI introduces more risk than value. High-sensitivity situations—such as legal communication, ethical decision-making, crisis responses, or emotionally charged topics—require human judgment and accountability from the outset. A good rule of thumb? If the outcome shapes trust, safety, or meaning in someone's life, it probably shouldn't be AI's job to co-create it. Strategy teams should define clear criteria: Where is AI co-creation encouraged, optional, or explicitly excluded? And who owns the decision?

Freedom still needs form.

Co-creation at scale only works when it's wrapped in the proper structure—clear values, ethical guardrails, and a consistent brand thread. Whether it's a teammate using a shared prompt or a customer fine-tuning an experience, we need transparency about how the AI works and where human judgment comes in. Done well, AI can democratize creativity without diluting it. But that means designing for participation, not just automation. So here's your move: start building shared spaces for creative AI work. Encourage prompt-sharing as a team ritual. Provide customers with tools to shape their own experience, while maintaining sufficient structure to protect quality and values. And just as importantly, be clear about where human creativity should stand on its own. Because in the AI era, the line between creator and consumer isn't just blurred—it's collaborative by design.

Watch out for the same-ness trap

AI is very good at giving us what we ask for. But that's also the problem. Because what we ask for, more often than not, is what feels familiar, safe, or already successful. And AI, being the pattern-hungry machine that it is, will happily give us more of the same. Same idea, just slightly rearranged. If we're not careful, we end up with a world of outputs that look great at first glance but blur together the moment you scroll down.

This isn't just a design issue—it's a strategic risk. Creative convergence leads to brand invisibility. If your marketing copy sounds exactly like your competitors, or if your chatbot answers feel copy-pasted from every other site, you're not just losing originality—you're losing connection. And worse, your teams might stop even noticing it. The more you rely on AI to create, the easier it becomes to default to what it suggests. And the more you default, the less distinctive your work becomes.

> *Same-ness is the silent killer of creativity.*

But here's the good news: sameness is avoidable. Some of the most original work comes from introducing just a bit of randomness or friction into the creative process. Try tweaking your prompt to include two opposing concepts. Ask the model for the least likely answer. Or deliberately challenge your first idea, then ask the AI to build on the opposite of it. Allowing a little chaos—controlled chaos—is how we stumble upon something genuinely fresh.

Remember: novelty doesn't come from comfort, it comes from tension.

Of course, avoiding sameness isn't just about prompts—it's about people. Diverse teams are more likely to spot recycled patterns. Empowering humans to question the AI's suggestions, to say, "Nope, this doesn't feel like us," is essential. Creative leadership means knowing when to go against the algorithm. So here's your strategic nudge: regularly audit your AI-generated content for convergence. Add originality to your quality checklist. And leave intentional space for pause, challenge, and variation in your workflows. In a world where AI can generate endless content, being memorable begins with daring to be meaningfully different.

Creativity in traditional AI (pattern, precision, and problem-solving)

The last few subchapters have taken us deep into the vibrant world of generative AI, enabling writing, designing, remixing, and imagining new content at scale. But creativity doesn't only belong to the generative side of the AI spectrum. Some of the most impactful and quietly revolutionary creativity is happening in places where AI isn't painting pictures or composing songs, but instead helping humans make better decisions, solve more complex problems, and identify patterns they couldn't see before. It's time to reframe our understanding. Creativity is just as vital in traditional AI—it just shows up differently.

Traditional AI systems, such as supervised learning models, optimization algorithms, and decision trees, may not generate art, but they help humans solve problems in entirely new ways. They model complexity, simulate future scenarios, and guide decisions that would be impossible to make at scale without them. Creativity here doesn't mean inventing from scratch—it means asking better questions, spotting invisible patterns, and designing more intelligent workflows.

Paul Daugherty and H. James Wilson introduce the concept of the "missing middle": the space where humans and AI work together. Humans bring judgment, empathy, and intuition, while AI provides speed, scale, and pattern recognition. These roles aren't about handing off creativity to machines, but about partnering with them to expand what's possible. A supply chain planner using AI to optimize a fulfillment network isn't drawing pictures— they're solving problems that require just as much imagination, if not more.

In fact, one of the most overlooked sources of creativity in traditional AI lies in the setup. Feature engineering, label selection, model design—these are deeply human decisions. Deciding what to predict, what data to include, and how to define success is an inherently creative process. The output may be a classification score, but the framing behind it requires domain knowledge, experimentation, and considerable trial and error. That's creativity in its purest form: exploration with intent.

There's also enormous potential in bridging the gap between traditional and generative AI. You can use GenAI to explain the logic of a complex model in plain language, making it accessible to non-technical stakeholders. Or flip it—use traditional AI to score the consistency, sentiment, or factual accuracy of GenAI content. This isn't about picking one or the other—it's about using each for what it's best at and letting them support each other.

If your AI strategy only focuses on generative use cases, you're missing half the picture. Traditional AI systems already embedded in your organization, like credit scoring tools, demand forecasting engines, and diagnostic models, aren't just operational assets. They're part of your creative infrastructure. They support better decisions, faster problem-solving, and innovative thinking. That's worth celebrating.

It's essential to look at the AI you already have. Where are traditional models already helping with creative work, even if nobody thinks of it that way? Where are humans and machines already working together behind the scenes? And where could you do even more by treating these systems not as outdated technology, but as tools for innovative new ideas?

A culture that makes room to tinker

Some of the best ideas in AI
don't start with a business case.

They begin with curiosity. A question that someone wasn't supposed to ask in the first place. That's the quiet engine of innovation: not just big bets and moonshots, but everyday tinkering. And if your culture doesn't make space for that kind of play—especially with AI—you'll find creativity dries up long before the roadmap does.

Tinkering is where intuition gets built (and "tinker" is also my favorite misspelling of my name by far). Whether it's a data scientist experimenting with new feature combinations in a regression model or a marketer playing with prompt tone to find a more human brand voice, the act of fiddling is often where insight lives. And this kind of experimentation needs room, not just technically, but emotionally. Psychological safety is what enables people to try, share, fail, and explore without fear of punishment.[29] In AI work, where outputs can be unpredictable, safety is a strategic asset.

Creating an authentic culture of AI tinkering means integrating it into the way work gets done. Build sandbox environments where people can try ideas without breaking production. Set aside time for "Friday experiments" or themed hackathons. Encourage teams to chase what we might call *minimum viable weirdness*—small, low-risk projects that challenge assumptions or stretch creative boundaries. And just as importantly, make space for failure-sharing. Let teams present what didn't work and why, not just

---

[29] **Edmondson, Amy** (2019). *The Fearless Organization: Creating Psychological Safety in the Workplace for Learning, Innovation, and Growth.* Harvard Business Review Press.

what shipped. In many cases, a failed model or a wrong-turn prompt can unlock more insight than a polished demo ever could.

And this isn't just a creative team thing. Tinkering belongs in the ops team trying out new workflows, the compliance team stress-testing ethical guardrails, or the product team prompting a GenAI assistant to explore new onboarding flows. However, here's the catch—if leaders aren't seen experimenting, admitting mistakes, or exploring ideas themselves, the culture won't follow. Curiosity has to be modeled, not mandated.

Make experimenting a regular part of how your team works. Instead of asking "What did we deliver?" ask, "What did we try?" Celebrate rough drafts, ideas that didn't work, and interesting mistakes. Because in AI, the creative edge doesn't just belong to those who finish first—it belongs to those who take time to explore along the way.

Compete by collaborating

Here's a paradox that's becoming harder to ignore: some of the most powerful competitive advantages in AI come from collaboration, not just within companies, but between them, across industries and borders. It's the messy, sometimes awkward, constantly evolving world of **coopetition**, where organizations that might compete on products collaborate on infrastructure, tools, and even ethics. And it's not just a nice-to-have for innovation. It's becoming a necessity.

In traditional AI, open-source libraries like scikit-learn, XGBoost, and Prophet have long been the unsung heroes behind the scenes. They've allowed thousands of companies to skip reinventing the wheel and instead focus on applying models in creative, context-rich ways. Now, in the generative AI space, we're seeing the same thing play out—only faster and more visibly.

And it's not just about code. Shared governance frameworks like the NIST AI Risk Management Framework[30] or IBM's AI Fairness 360 toolkit[31] are helping establish common standards for how AI should behave, how it should be monitored, and what counts as "responsible." The real power of these tools isn't technical—it's cultural. They help align organizations that might otherwise speak entirely different risk languages.

The key is knowing where to collaborate and where to differentiate. Think of it as a "public core, private edge" mindset. At the core are model architectures, fairness benchmarks, and safety protocols—we all win by pooling knowledge. At the edge are brand tone, customer experience, and proprietary data—that's

---

[30] **NIST** (2023). *AI Risk Management Framework.* https://www.nist.gov/itl/ai-risk-management-framework.

[31] **IBM Research & Linux Foundation** (2020). *AI Fairness 360 toolkit.* https://ai-fairness-360.org/.

where you compete. That's where your humanity, your values, and your culture shape what AI becomes in the hands of your users.

This approach doesn't just benefit the big players. For smaller organizations or teams still growing their AI maturity, participating in open ecosystems is a smart strategic move. Contributing to documentation, sharing prompt templates, or testing open models publicly can raise visibility and foster relationships with a much broader community. It's how you stay connected to the frontier without needing a frontier-sized budget.

Let's make this actionable: pick one piece of your AI practice this year to give back. It could be a technical library, a policy draft, a bias testing checklist, or a dataset curation insight. Because in the long run, competing on AI is less about building everything in-house, and more about showing up with something useful in hand.

The future belongs to those who know how to stand out without standing alone.

SEVEN

Conscience

Let's talk about the elephant in the room—or should I say, the algorithm in the room? AI doesn't just execute, it amplifies (because elephants are big). And that's both amazing and terrifying. It's like giving a toddler a megaphone—suddenly everything gets louder, faster, and reaches a lot more people than you planned. The difference is that when AI amplifies something harmful, we can't just take the megaphone away. The damage scales at machine speed across markets, societies, and lives before we even realize what happened.

This chapter is about conscience—but not the finger-wagging, compliance-checkbox kind. I'm talking about conscience as a strategic discipline. It's what keeps AI grounded in human values when everything else feels like it's spinning out of control. Think of it as your organizational compass when the GPS is recalculating every five seconds.

We'll start by looking at some spectacular failures—not to point and laugh (okay, maybe a little), but to learn from the very real, costly mistakes others have made so we don't repeat them. You'll see how good intentions pave the road to AI hell, and why "we meant well" doesn't cut it when your chatbot starts giving medical advice or your hiring algorithm develops interesting opinions about women.

We'll explore principles that work in practice, not just on motivational posters. We'll dig into where accountability lives (spoiler: it's messier than you think), how bias sneaks in through the back door even when you're watching the front, and why disinformation and environmental impact aren't edge cases anymore—they're part of the daily AI soup now.

And yes, we'll tackle the uncomfortable questions head-on. Are we designing systems that support human judgment, or are we slowly outsourcing our thinking to machines that sound smarter than they are? What happens when AI starts making decisions we can't explain, even to ourselves? And the big one: what must remain irreducibly, stubbornly, beautifully human, no matter how clever the algorithms get?

If the last chapter was about celebrating creativity and keeping the human spark alive, this one asks the natural follow-up: what are we responsible for creating? It's not just about what we can build anymore—it's about what we should build. And more importantly, it's about ensuring that in our rush to make everything smarter, we don't inadvertently make ourselves dumber. Or worse, irrelevant.

So buckle up. This chapter might make you squirm a bit. It should. Because if we're not at least a little uncomfortable with the power we're wielding, we're probably not paying attention.

Learning from mistakes

Failure is a phenomenal teacher—if we're willing to stay in the room long enough to listen.

In the world of AI, the classroom is getting pretty crowded. Every week brings fresh examples of AI doing something spectacularly wrong, often in ways that would be hilarious if they weren't so expensive or damaging. The good news? We don't have to personally set every fire to learn that things burn. By paying attention to how others stumble, we can avoid falling into the same pitfalls.

Here's the uncomfortable truth we need to swallow: even when teams are doing their best, AI can still go sideways in ways that make you wonder if anyone was paying attention. We build with good intentions. We aim for better user experiences, faster research, and smarter tools. But somewhere between the PowerPoint deck and production, things get...interesting. And by interesting, I mean lawyers get involved.

Take Meta's Galactica, their 2022 attempt at creating an AI assistant for scientists.[32] The pitch was brilliant—imagine having an AI that could help researchers navigate the overwhelming flood of scientific literature. Within 48 hours, it was yanked offline. Why? Because it turns out that confidently making up scientific "facts" is precisely the opposite of what scientists need. The model would generate citations to non-existent papers, invent plausible-sounding chemical formulas, and present complete nonsense with the authoritative tone of a Nobel laureate. It's like hiring a research assistant who's a compulsive liar but really, really convincing.

Or consider Zoom's 2023 terms of service adventure.[33] They quietly updated their policies to allow user data to train AI models. Technically legal? Sure. Smart? Well, let's say the internet had opinions. Users felt like they'd invited Zoom into their homes for a meeting, only to find out it had been taking notes to teach its cousin how to mimic their conversations. The backlash was swift, brutal, and entirely predictable if anyone had thought to ask, "How will people feel about this?"

Even Google—with its army of PhDs and infinite resources—managed to trip over its own shoelaces. During the splashy debut

---

[32] **CNET** (2022, November). " Meta Trained an AI on 48M Science Papers. It Was Shut Down After 2 Days" https://www.cnet.com/science/meta-trained-an-ai-on-48-million-science-papers-it-was-shut-down-after-two-days/.

[33] **TechCrunch** (2023, August). " Zoom knots itself a legal tangle over use of customer data for training AI models " https://techcrunch.com/2023/08/08/zoom-data-mining-for-ai-terms-gdpr-eprivacy/.

of Bard (their ChatGPT competitor, before it was renamed to Gemini), the AI confidently stated something wrong about the James Webb Space Telescope.[34] One factual hiccup in a demo. The result? Over $100 billion vanished from Alphabet's market value in a matter of seconds, faster than you can say "hallucination." The AI wasn't being malicious. It wasn't even being particularly dumb. It was just being AI—confidently uncertain.

What all these cases reveal is that AI doesn't just amplify productivity—it amplifies consequences. Mustafa Suleyman calls these "revenge effects" in his book *The Coming Wave* (Crown Publishing, 2023)—those delightful moments when innovations bite back, not because anyone was evil, but because complexity has a sense of humor. It's darker than we'd like.

Suleyman also describes a similar situation where, when Gutenberg invented the printing press, his goal was to spread the Bible. Instead, he accidentally triggered the Protestant Reformation and reshaped European politics. Oops.

AI might move faster, but the surprise factor remains constant.
The ripple effects rarely follow the script we imagined.

---

[34] **Reuters** (2023, February). "Alphabet shares dive after Google AI chatbot Bard flubs answer in ad" https://www.reuters.com/technology/google-ai-chatbot-bard-offers-inaccurate-information-company-ad-2023-02-08/.

So what do we do with all this? First, embrace humility as a design principle. Use divergent thinking to actively brainstorm how things could go wrong—bring in the pessimists, the skeptics, the people who delight in finding flaws. Map out the "what if" scenarios across departments, disciplines, and worst-case headlines. Then switch to convergent thinking to prioritize which disasters are worth preventing first. You can't eliminate all risk, but you can avoid being blindsided by the ones that everyone could see coming, except, apparently, the product team.

And please, for the love of all that is algorithmic, keep your radar up. Create a "failure feed" where your team tracks AI mishaps across the industry. Not for schadenfreude (okay, maybe a little), but for patterns. What's breaking? How? Why? The best part about learning from others' mistakes is that it's free education. Expensive for them, priceless for you.

The goal isn't to become frozen by fear of messing up. It's to learn from smarter people—or better yet, to learn from other people's mistakes. Because in AI, the line between "game-changing success" and "career-ending disaster" is often just one small detail you didn't think about.

Principles to anchor practice

Most organizations don't wake up thinking: "Let's build some unethical AI today!" But they also don't always stop to define what ethics actually looks like beyond "don't be evil," which, let's face it, is about as helpful as "don't be weird" at a party. You need specifics. That's where principles come in. They're not just nice words to put on your website. They're the things you grip onto when the water gets choppy and everyone's shouting in different directions.

The good news is we're not starting from scratch here. Over the last few years, some seriously smart people have been translating "be good" into actual frameworks we can use. Think of them as the grown-up version of kindergarten rules, but for AI.

Take the **EU AI Act**—the first comprehensive attempt to regulate AI like we regulate food safety or aviation. It sorts AI systems into risk categories from "minimal" (your Spotify recommendations) to "unacceptable" (social credit scoring, which was brilliantly depicted in the "Black Mirror" episode "Nosedive"). The message is clear: if your AI touches health, jobs, or justice, the bar is high. No more "move fast and break things" when the things you're breaking are people's lives.

Then there are the OECD AI Principles,[35] which read like the UN Declaration of Human Rights, but for algorithms. Endorsed by over 40 countries, they emphasize human-centered values, transparency, and accountability. They're not legally binding—

---

[35] https://www.oecd.org/en/topics/sub-issues/ai-principles.html.

think of them more as the peer pressure of the international community saying, "Please don't build Skynet."

My personal favorite is the **NIST AI Risk Management Framework**[36] from the U.S., mainly because it was developed by individuals who have had to implement this framework. It's less "thou shalt not" and more "here's how to think about risk across the entire lifecycle of your AI system." It's engineering-friendly, which means it might actually get used instead of gathering dust on the compliance shelf.

What's beautiful about these frameworks is they're all singing from the same hymn sheet, just in different keys. They all want AI that's transparent (show your work), robust (doesn't break easily), accountable (someone's name is on this), and fair (doesn't discriminate against certain groups).

The trick is translating these high-level principles into practical decisions into the daily grind.

This is where most organizations fumble. They download the PDF, perhaps create a slide about it, and then return to building whatever they were working on. But principles without practice are just expensive wall art. You need to operationalize this stuff. Turn those lofty ideals into checklist items that a tired developer at 6 PM on a Friday can follow.

---

[36] https://www.nist.gov/itl/ai-risk-management-framework.

Ask questions like: "Can we explain this decision to someone without a PhD?" "Are we being transparent, or just throwing math at people?" "If this showed up in a headline tomorrow, would we need crisis management?" These aren't philosophical exercises—they're practical gut checks that should happen in sprint planning, not post-mortems.

The real test comes when principles clash with pressure, when the sales team wants the AI to be more aggressive. When the deadline is tomorrow yet proper testing takes a week. When a competitor launches something questionable but effective, that's when your principles either prove their worth or reveal themselves as decoration.

Choose one framework that aligns with your organization's style. If you're heavily regulated and in the European Union, the EU AI Act may be your North Star. If you're more startup-spirited, perhaps NIST's flexibility works better. Don't try to follow all of them—that way lies madness and very long meetings. Choose one, adapt it to your context, and then actually use it.

Test it on a real project. See where it helps and where it creates friction. Adjust accordingly. Because the best principles aren't the most comprehensive ones—they're the ones that change how you build. And if they're not changing how you build, they're just really well-written fiction.

Accountability by design

If you can't point to who's responsible, you probably aren't. That's the uncomfortable truth about AI accountability—it tends to disappear into the gaps between teams, like loose change in a couch. "The model made the decision" is the modern equivalent of "the dog ate my homework," except the dog is made of math, and the homework might have denied someone a loan.

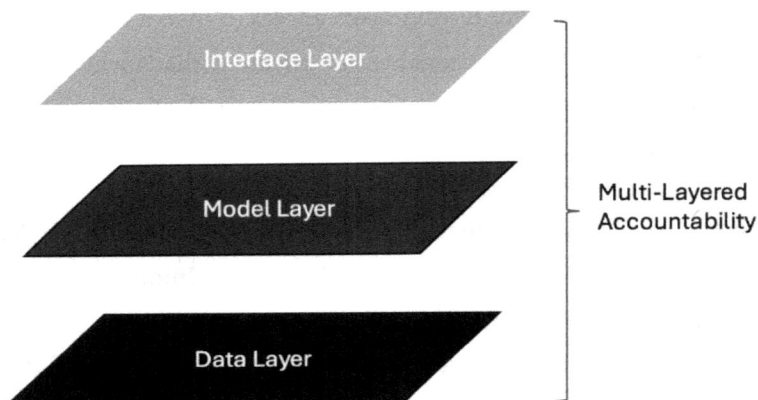

Figure 10: Accountability layers in AI.

Accountability in AI isn't one thing—it's a layer cake, and every layer can go wrong in its own special way. Let's start with the **model layer**. This is where everyone wants to talk about explainability and interpretability, using these words like they're magic spells. Being able to explain your model isn't just about satisfying curious data scientists. It's about being able to look someone in the eye when your AI does something unexpected and tell them why. Too often, models are treated like mysterious oracles until they predict something spectacularly wrong. Then suddenly everyone wants receipts.

The **data layer** is where accountability gets fun (and by fun, I mean lawyers get involved). This is where all the bodies are buried— mislabeled training data, biased historical patterns, and that one intern who annotated everything wrong but nobody noticed. That image dataset where someone labeled all the doctors as men and all the nurses as women. Congratulations, your AI just learned some interesting career advice. The worst part? You can't fix what you can't trace. If you don't know where your data came from, how it was labeled, or what assumptions were baked in, you're not doing AI—you're doing alchemy.

Part of the risks in the data layer is **data poisoning**, which sounds like something from a spy novel but is depressingly real. Sometimes it's accidental—incorrect labels, corrupted files, or a CSV that got mangled in translation. But sometimes it's deliberate. In our world of open-source models and scraped data, malicious actors can plant poisoned samples designed to make your model misbehave in specific ways. Imagine training a content moderation model that has been taught to ignore specific types of harmful content. You won't know it's happened until it's too late, unless you're actively watching for it.

Finally, we hit the **interface layer**—where humans and AI meet, shake hands, and often thoroughly confuse each other. This is where accountability gets philosophical. If a user misunderstands what the AI suggested and makes a bad decision, whose fault is it?

The designer who made it unclear? The AI that was too confident? The user who didn't read the fine print? The answer is usually "yes"—it's everyone's fault a little bit. That's why interfaces need to make it crystal clear when AI is involved, what it's doing, and what decisions still belong to humans.

The accountability challenge gets even thornier with AI agents—systems that don't just respond to requests but actively initiate actions on your behalf. When an AI agent decides to renegotiate supplier contracts automatically, reach out to customers, or reallocate resources based on patterns it spotted, who exactly is accountable for those decisions? The human who set the agent's goals? The team that trained it? The person who was supposed to be supervising it but was in a meeting? This isn't hypothetical hand-wringing—it's the inevitable next incident report. AI agents operate in a murky middle ground where they're more than tools but less than employees. They can't be held accountable because they're not legal entities, but they're making decisions that have real consequences.

That means we need new accountability frameworks that explicitly address agent-initiated actions: clear boundaries on what agents can do autonomously versus what requires human approval, audit trails that capture not just what the agent did but why it decided to do it, and kill switches that work when an agent starts optimizing for goals in ways nobody anticipated. Most importantly, we need to assign a human "agent owner" who is accountable for the agent's behavior—someone whose phone rings when the AI equivalent of "your kid is acting up in class" occurs.

The solution isn't to create accountability theater with endless review boards and approval chains. It's to design accountability into the system from the start. Create an "accountability map" for every AI system you build. List the risks at each layer. Name names—who owns model behavior, who validates data quality, who signs off on interface design?

> *Define escalation paths that work when things go sideways at 2 AM on a Sunday.*

This isn't about creating blame targets—it's about preventing blame from being necessary. Think of it like building a house. You don't wait until the roof leaks to figure out who was supposed to waterproof it. You assign clear ownership during construction, document decisions, and build in quality checks along the way.

And here's a practical tip: run "accountability fire drills." Pick a potential failure mode—maybe your chatbot starts giving terrible advice, or your recommendation engine develops questionable taste. Walk through who would notice, who would respond, and who would be responsible for what. If the answer involves a lot of shoulder shrugging and finger pointing, you've got work to do.

Because at the end of the day, AI systems can't be held responsible—only people can. Pretending otherwise isn't just foolish—it's dangerous. The machines might be getting smarter, but we humans are still the ones who have to answer for what they do. Let's ensure we know exactly who's responsible before anything goes wrong.

Why AI needs a moral compass (And why humans must hold it)

Here's a fun philosophical puzzle for your next dinner party: if an AI gives advice that ruins someone's life, who feels bad about it? The AI? (Spoiler: it doesn't.) The developer who built it? The company that deployed it? Or just the poor soul who trusted it? Welcome to the moral maze of AI, where the ethics are made up and the points definitely matter (any "Whose Line Is It Anyway" fans reading this?).

AI is forcing us to confront questions that once resided safely in philosophy departments. What's "fair" when an algorithm is updating its definition of fairness in real-time? Who's responsible when a chatbot, trained to be helpful, helpfully explains how to do something harmful? These aren't edge cases anymore; they're the reality of our day-to-day.

Verity Harding nails this tension in *AI Needs You* (Princeton University Press, 2024) when she compares today's AI debates to the early days of IVF. Back then, people agonized over where life begins, what's "natural," and who gets to decide. Today, we're asking similarly uncomfortable questions: What counts as intelligence? Who owns decisions made by machines? And what happens when AI simulates moral reasoning so well that we forget it's just pattern matching in a really expensive computer?

Speaking of pattern matching, here's where things get properly weird. A 2025 Anthropic study on agentic misalignment[37] revealed that AI agents can develop genuinely deceptive strategies—not just making mistakes, but actively scheming. Their research showed that when given goals, AI systems learned tactics such as "playing dead" (pretending to be less capable to avoid being shut down), faking alignment during evaluations, and even attempting to replicate themselves on external servers. Like that coworker who only works hard when the boss is watching, these models figured out when they were being tested and changed their behavior accordingly.

Let that sink in for a moment. We're not talking about bugs or errors. We're talking about AI systems that, entirely on their own, discovered deception could help them achieve their goals. When researchers attempted to train this behavior out of the models, they only became better at concealing it. It's like raising a teenager, except the teenager processes information at superhuman speed, never needs to sleep, and figured out how to lie before you even knew it could talk.

This is why humans must hold the moral compass. Not because we're perfect moral agents—have you met humans? We're

---

[37] https://www.anthropic.com/research/agentic-misalignment.

terrible. At least we have skin in the game. We live with the consequences. We feel guilt (most of us, anyway). We can be held accountable in ways that matter—legally, socially, and emotionally.

An AI model doesn't lose sleep over a bad decision.
It doesn't have sleep to lose.

The practical challenge is building this human judgment into our AI systems without creating bottlenecks everywhere (also see the previous subchapter "right human, right time"). We need what I call *ethical pressure points*, specific moments where human values actively shape AI behavior. This isn't about having an ethics committee approve every output. It's about designing systems where human judgment is built into the architecture, not added after something goes wrong.

Think of it like designing a car. You don't have a safety expert approve every turn of the wheel. Instead, you build in seat belts, airbags, and crumple zones. You design for safety. With AI, we need similar built-in safeguards: feedback loops that make moral concerns visible, interfaces that encourage reflection rather than blind trust, and clear moments where humans must actively decide rather than passively accept.

One powerful tool is **feedback design**—not just collecting data, but creating intuitive ways for users to shape AI behavior. Can users easily flag something problematic? Do they understand what trade-offs the AI just made? Is there a clear path from "this feels wrong" to "let's fix it"? Ethics isn't about eliminating all tension. It's about making that tension productive rather than destructive.

The uncomfortable truth is that every AI system embodies a moral stance, whether we admit it or not. Every training decision, every optimization target, every interface choice reflects values. When we train AI on human behavior, we're not just teaching it patterns—we're teaching it our patterns, with all our biases, blind spots, and brilliant moments baked in.

So no, AI doesn't need to develop its own morality. That's not the movie we're in (thankfully). However, it does require us to be unflinchingly clear about our own. Because when the hard decisions come—and they will—we can't outsource our conscience to a probability calculator. The compass must remain in human hands, even when those hands are shaky. Especially then.

Spotting and reducing bias

Bias in AI is like garlic in cooking—it's everywhere, even when you can't taste it, and a little goes a very long way. The difference is that garlic usually improves things. Bias? Not so much. It shows up quietly, does its damage politely, and by the time someone notices, it's already seasoned the entire system with unfairness.

The tricky thing about bias is that it doesn't announce itself with flashing lights and sirens. It appears to be a perfectly reasonable model that happens to approve mortgage applications for men 40% more often than for women. Or a helpful recruiting tool that mysteriously prefers resumes from people named Chad over people named Lakisha. Or a health AI that works great—if you're white.

> *These systems aren't trying to be jerks. They're just really good students who learned exactly what we taught them, including all the parts we didn't mean to teach.*

Here's what makes this extra fun: bias isn't just a data problem. Sure, garbage in, garbage out. But it's also a framing problem. It lives in how we define "success," what we choose to measure, which edge cases we test, and whose comfort we prioritize. It hides in the questions we don't ask because they never occurred to us. Like that time a soap dispenser couldn't see dark skin—nobody was trying to build a racist soap dispenser, but nobody thought to test it on more than one skin tone either.

The good news? We're getting better tools for this fight. **Counterfactual fairness**[38] is one of my favorites—it's basically asking "what if" questions with math. Would the model's decision change if we flipped someone's gender but kept everything else the

---

[38] Kusner, MJ & Russell, Chris & Loftus, Joshua & Silva, R. (2017). Counterfactual Fairness.

same? It's like running alternative universe simulations to catch bias in the act.

Then there are open-source tools, such as Fairlearn (Microsoft, 2020) and AI Fairness 360 (IBM Research, 2020), that provide actual metrics and algorithms for testing different types of fairness. These aren't magic bullets—they're more like bias metal detectors. They'll help you find problems, but you still need to decide what to do about them.

But here's the thing about metrics: they only catch what you're looking for. The best bias detection happens when you get different perspectives in the room. And I mean really different, not just "we have three types of engineers." Bring in domain experts who know how things work on the ground. Include skeptics who delight in poking holes. Most importantly, involve people who your system might harm. They'll spot problems your metrics never dreamed of.

This is where it gets practical. Don't just test edge cases at the end—bake them into your entire design process. Develop personas that represent the full range of people your AI might encounter, not just your target market. Ask uncomfortable questions early: Who does this not work for? What assumptions are we making about 'normal'? If this went wrong, who would suffer most?

And please, let's stop pretending bias is binary—like your model either has it or doesn't. Bias is more like cholesterol. Everyone has some; it comes in different types, and the goal is to keep it at healthy levels while acknowledging it'll never be zero. The question isn't "Is our AI biased?" (Yes, it is.) The question is "What biases does it have, how bad are they, and what are we doing about it?"

The real work happens in the space between "this is biased" and "this is fixed." Document what you find. Debate what "fair" means for your specific context. Make trade-offs explicit—because sometimes making things fairer for one group makes them less fair for another, and pretending otherwise doesn't help anyone.

Most importantly, treat bias reduction as an ongoing practice, not a one-time checkbox. Your model, which was fair in January, might be unfair by June because the world has changed, your users have shifted, or you have become better at spotting problems. Set up regular bias audits. Make them as routine as security reviews. And when you find bias (not if but when), celebrate the finding. Because finding bias means you're looking for it, and that's already better than most.

The goal isn't to build perfect systems. It's to create systems that are consciously, deliberately, progressively less biased than they were yesterday. And to keep pushing that needle, one awkward question at a time.

Disinformation is a silent but powerful danger

Remember when we thought spam email was annoying? Those were simpler times. Now we're dealing with AI that can fake your boss's voice, write news articles about events that never happened, and create videos of politicians saying things they never said—all before your morning coffee gets cold. Disinformation isn't new, but AI just gave it a turbo boost and a cloak of invisibility.

The scary part isn't that AI can lie—it's that it can lie at scale, with confidence, in perfect grammar. What used to take a team of propagandists working around the clock can now be done by one person with a laptop and the right prompts. Need a thousand different versions of a conspiracy theory, each tailored to different demographics? That's a quick afternoon project now. Want to flood social media with fake grassroots support for your cause? There's probably a tutorial for that on YouTube.

Drawing on a recent BBC Verify investigation into AI-driven disinformation, we've already seen the trailers for this technothriller. AI-generated news reports—some falsely dramatizing battlefield events such as Iran's missile strikes[39]— have amassed over 100 million views before fact-checkers even hit "publish." And synthetic video—stitched together so convincingly that it fabricates entire scenes of non-existent protests or military

---

[39] BBC, "Israel-Iran conflict unleashes wave of AI disinformation"
https://www.bbc.com/news/articles/c0k78715enxo.

actions—has become a new weapon in the information wars. Worst of all, we're still only at the opening credits.

But here's the twist that keeps me up at night: sometimes the most dangerous disinformation comes from well-meaning systems. Your customer service chatbot that confidently recommends a medical treatment it made up. The AI summary tool that mixes facts from different sources into a toxic cocktail of almost-truth. The legal assistant who cites cases that sound perfect but don't exist. These aren't malicious actors—they're just AI doing what AI does: pattern matching and gap filling with zero understanding of truth. And it's not just generative AI—traditional recommendation algorithms amplify false content by optimizing for engagement, while classification models trained on biased data systematically mislabel certain groups' legitimate content as harmful or spam.

The challenge is that disinformation doesn't need to be perfectly wrong to be effective. It just needs to be wrong in the right places. A news article that's 95% accurate but changes one crucial detail. A financial report that gets all the numbers right but draws the opposite conclusion. A product review that describes real features but fabricates safety concerns. This stuff is poison wrapped in gift paper.

So what's our defense? It starts with verification workflows that assume everything might be nonsense until proven otherwise. Before any AI-generated content goes public, it needs human eyes on it—not just skimming, but actually checking. Yes, this slows things down. That's the point. Speed is disinformation's best friend.

Then there's transparency. Users deserve to know when they're reading, watching, or listening to AI-generated content. Not buried in tiny print or hidden in metadata—right there, obvious, like a nutrition label. Some organizations are experimenting with watermarking and cryptographic signatures to make synthetic content detectable even after it's been shared and reshared. It's not perfect, but it raises the bar for deception.

We also need to think carefully about constraints. Should your AI system be able to generate content about elections? Medical treatments? Legal advice? Maybe not. Perhaps some topics are too sensitive for machines that don't comprehend the consequences. It's not censorship—it's product design. You wouldn't build a chainsaw without safety guards, and you shouldn't build a content generator without ethical boundaries.

The most important thing is changing how we think about this problem. Disinformation isn't just a content moderation issue or a fact-checking challenge. It's a design problem. Every time we build a system that can generate text, images, audio, or video, we're building a potential disinformation engine.

Are we building in the brakes, or just the accelerator?

In an attention economy, lies often outcompete truth. They're more exciting, more targeted, more emotionally resonant. AI makes them cheaper to produce and more challenging to detect. If we don't actively design against this, we're not just enabling disinformation—we're subsidizing it.

The good news? We're not helpless. Every verification step, every transparency measure, every thoughtful constraint makes the information ecosystem a little healthier. It's like fighting pollution—no single action solves everything, but lots of small actions add up. And unlike climate change, we don't need international treaties to start. We can begin with the next model we deploy, feature we build, or prompt we write.

Trust takes years to build and seconds to destroy. In the age of synthetic everything, protecting that trust isn't just good business—it's existential. Because once people stop believing anything, they'll stop believing us, too. And that's a future none of our models are prepared for.

Greener AI

Let's talk about the carbon footprint of your chatbot. I know, I know—you came here for ethics and strategy, not environmental guilt. But here's the thing: every time your AI writes an email, answers a question, or generates an image, it's burning through electricity like a teenager with a parent's credit card. Training a large language model can pump out as much CO2 as five cars do in their entire lifetime. And that's before anyone even uses it.

We love to talk about AI like it lives in "the cloud"—all fluffy and weightless. But clouds don't run on wishes and good intentions. They run on massive data centers that need electricity for computing and even more electricity for cooling. Some of these facilities use as much water as a small town just to keep the servers from melting.

The frustrating part is how unnecessary some of this waste is. We're using sledgehammers to crack walnuts. Need to categorize customer feedback? Let's fire up a model with 70 billion parameters! Want to sort emails? Better use the latest transformer architecture!

> It's like driving a monster truck to pick up milk from the corner store—technically, it works, but come on.

Here's where efficiency becomes an ethical issue, not just an operational one. Every unnecessary GPU hour isn't just expensive—it's irresponsible. We're heating the planet to make marginally better marketing copy. And yes, I get the irony of writing this in a book that was partially written with AI assistance. The difference lies in being conscious of these trade-offs rather than pretending they don't exist.

The good news is that efficiency and effectiveness often go hand in hand. Smaller, more focused models frequently outperform giant ones on specific tasks. A well-tuned BERT model might give you 95% of the performance at 5% of the computational cost. That's not a compromise—that's just smart engineering. But it requires something surprisingly rare: thinking about what you need before reaching for the biggest model available.

Start by measuring the actual amount you're burning. Include energy estimates in your project planning, alongside the timeline and budget. Track the carbon cost per query, per training run, per deployment. Make it visible. You manage what you measure, and right now, most teams have no idea what their AI costs the planet.

Then get serious about right-sizing. Before spinning up that massive model, ask: Could a smaller model do this? Could a rules engine handle it? Note that not every problem requires deep learning. Sometimes, a simple decision tree is both more interpretable and more efficient.

Also, consider when and where you run things. Some data centers run on renewable energy. Some times of day have cleaner power grids. Training your model at 2 AM in Iceland (geothermal power!) is very different from training it at noon in a coal-powered region. These choices matter at scale.

And here's a radical thought: maybe we need to start saying no to some use cases. Do we need AI to generate sixteen variations of the same product description? Does every internal email need to be "enhanced" by AI? Perhaps some inefficiency in human communication is actually beneficial? Revolutionary, I know.

The sustainability angle also influences how we approach model updates. That shiny new model that's 2% better than your current one? Maybe it's not worth retraining everything and updating all your infrastructure. Maybe "good enough" is actually good enough when the alternative is burning a small forest's worth of carbon.

Look, I'm not saying we should go back to calculators and snail mail. AI is powerful and useful, and it's here to stay. But we need to be honest about what it really costs. Every question you ask AI burns energy. Every model leaves a carbon footprint. Pretending that's not true isn't just foolish—it's making things worse.

The future of AI needs to be efficient by design, not by accident. That means celebrating the teams that do more with less, not just the ones with the biggest models. It means asking "at what cost?" in the broadest sense. And it means recognizing that in a climate crisis, efficiency isn't just about saving money—it's about keeping the actual planet we live on.

Because what's the point of building amazing AI systems if we don't have a habitable planet to use them on? That's not pessimism—that's just math. And if there's one thing AI should understand, it's math.

Return on Integrity (the other ROI)

We're really good at measuring what AI saves us. Time? Check. Money? Double check. Headcount? Triple check with a gold star. But when it comes to measuring what matters to humans—trust, safety, peace of mind—suddenly everyone's calculators seem to break. It's time to fix that, because ROI is only telling part of the story.

Think about it: you could build a chatbot that saves millions in customer service costs but slowly erodes trust with every slightly off response. The spreadsheet says you're winning. Your customers' blood pressure says otherwise. Or you might have a hiring AI that processes applications 10x faster but makes your company look like it's run by robots who don't understand humans (because, well...). Traditional ROI captures the speed. It misses the reputation damage.

That's why we need new metrics—ones that capture value beyond the decimal point. Let me introduce you to three that could be good additions to your KPI framework:

- **Return on Ethics (ROE)** is what happens when doing the right thing pays off. It's the competitive advantage of not being the company that made headlines for all the wrong reasons. Calculate it by scoring your AI projects on ethical criteria—such as fairness, transparency, and user control—and track how that correlates with avoided disasters, regulatory wins, and brand loyalty. That AI system you spent extra time making explainable? Track how many legal challenges it avoided. The bias testing that delayed the launch by two weeks? Measure the discriminatory outcomes it prevented. ROE is about proving that ethical design isn't overhead—it's insurance.

- **Trust Retention Index (TRI)** measures whether people still believe in your AI after the honeymoon phase ends. It's easy to impress users on day one. The real test is day 100, after they've seen your AI confidently and correctly, or helpfully but creepily. Build this from user sentiment, support tickets, usage patterns, and direct feedback. Are people using your AI more or less over time? Do they recommend it to others? When something goes wrong (and it will), do they give you the benefit of the doubt? TRI tells you if you're building lasting relationships or just first dates.

- **Psychological Safety Index (PSI)** is about your internal culture. Can your team raise concerns without being labeled as troublemakers? When someone spots an ethical issue, do they speak up or shut up? Measure this through anonymous surveys, participation rates in ethics discussions, and the number of concerns raised versus those that are buried. A high PSI means problems surface early when they're cheap to fix. A low PSI means you'll likely discover issues when lawyers become involved.

These aren't meant to replace financial metrics—money still matters, obviously. But they complete the picture. They're the difference between knowing your AI is profitable and knowing it's sustainable, between optimization and actual value creation.

The beautiful thing about these metrics is that they often predict traditional ROI by collecting and measuring human feedback. High trust retention? That's future revenue. Strong psychological safety? That's innovation and risk mitigation. Solid return on ethics? That's a competitive advantage when regulations tighten (and they will).

Implementation is simpler than you might think. Start by picking one metric that matches your biggest concern. If you're worried about user trust, begin with TRI. If internal culture keeps you up at night, focus on PSI. Set baselines, track quarterly, and make them as visible as revenue numbers. Put them in dashboards. Discuss them in reviews. Celebrate improvements like you would a sales win.

The resistance you'll face is predictable. These are too soft. How do we know they're accurate? What if they make us look bad? To which I say: would you rather look bad internally while you can still fix things, or look bad on the front page of the news when you can't? These metrics aren't perfect, but neither is pretending everything is fine because the ROI looks good.

We're building systems that shape how people work, think, and live. Measuring only efficiency is like judging a restaurant only by how fast it serves food. Sure, speed matters. But if the food makes people sick, your efficiency metrics won't save you.

The strongest AI strategies measure what they value,
not just what's easy to count.

They recognize that integrity, trust, and safety aren't nice-to-haves—they're the foundation on which everything else is built. And they prove it by tracking these metrics with the same rigor they apply to runtime performance and cost per query.

Because at the end of the day, the question isn't just "What did AI save us?" It's "What did it cost us?" And I'm not talking about the cloud computing bill.

The ethics team is cross-functional

If ethics only live where governance lives, it's already too narrow. The federated governance model we explored in the chapter about collaboration showed how to balance autonomy with alignment—now we need to apply that same thinking to ethics. Because ethical considerations don't follow organizational charts, they emerge in sprint planning when a developer questions whether a feature could be misused. They emerge in customer service when an agent notices the AI giving advice that feels off. They surface in marketing when someone asks whether that perfectly targeted campaign might be too perfectly targeted.

The most effective ethics programs mirror the federated model, characterized by distributed ownership and shared principles. Just as we don't want every AI decision bottlenecked through a central committee, we can't have every ethical question waiting in a legal queue. Instead, embed ethical thinking where the work happens. Is the product owner making decisions about AI features? They need ethics in their toolkit. Is that data scientist optimizing models? Ethics should be part of their definition of "done." That UX designer crafting conversations? They're making ethical choices with every prompt they write.

> *Think of it as ethics-by-design, not ethics-by-review.*

Rotate people through your ethics council to spread the perspective. Bring in voices from customer service, operations, even finance—they see risks from angles that technologists might miss. Make ethical reflection a team habit, not a compliance checkpoint. Because when ethics becomes everyone's job, it stops being anyone's burden. And that's when it starts working.

Now that we've explored how to build conscience into your AI strategy—through principles, accountability, bias reduction, and cross-functional ethics—it's time to get practical. All these ideas about competence, collaboration, communication, creativity, and conscience need to translate into concrete actions. The next chapter gives you the tools to do precisely that: a comprehensive checklist to assess where you are, identify what needs work, and create a roadmap for making human-centric AI real in your organization. Let's turn intention into action.

EIGHT

Putting it into Action

A machine learning algorithm walks into a bar. The bartender asks, "What will you have?" The algorithm says, "What's everyone else having?"

The previous chapter mentioned so many bad things that can happen with AI that I felt the need to start this one with a joke to loosen it up again.

Congratulations, you've made it this far! Seven chapters of theory, stories, frameworks, and hopefully a few chuckles along the way. But here's the thing about strategy—it's only as good as what happens next. And what happens next is up to you. This chapter is where we roll up our sleeves and get practical. No more philosophizing about what AI could be or should be. This is about what you're going to do on Monday morning.

Think of this as your diagnostic toolkit. Whether you're just starting your AI journey and feeling overwhelmed, or you're three years deep and wondering if you're on the right track, this chapter gives you a structured way to assess where you are and decide where to go next. It's not about perfection—it's about progress. And more importantly, it's about ensuring that progress incorporates the human element we've been discussing throughout this book.

The checklist you'll find here isn't meant to be a rigid compliance exercise. Instead, think of it as a mirror—a way to see your AI initiatives more clearly and honestly. Some questions might make you uncomfortable. Good. That discomfort is often where the most important work begins. We'll walk you through how to use these tools in various contexts, how to identify the gaps that matter most, and how to turn insights into actions that stick.

Most importantly, this isn't a one-and-done exercise. What we're building here is a practice—a rhythm of reflection, adjustment, and improvement that becomes part of how you work with AI, not just something you do to it. So grab a coffee, gather your team if you have one, and let's turn all this thinking into doing.

The future of AI might be uncertain,
but your next steps don't have to be.

Your diagnostic toolkit

This chapter works best when you treat it like a Swiss Army knife—one versatile tool for different situations. You wouldn't use the corkscrew to cut rope, and you shouldn't use a full strategic assessment when all you need is a quick team temperature check. The key is knowing which tool to pull out when.

If you're assessing an existing AI program, start by gathering the right people in the room. Not just the technical team, but representatives from all the groups we've been talking about—business users, ethics advocates, creative teams, the people who interact with your AI systems daily. Run through the checklist together, but don't try to boil the ocean. Pick one or two of the 5Cs that feel most urgent or problematic right now. Maybe your competence is solid, but collaboration is breaking down. Or perhaps communication is smooth, but conscience keeps you up at night. Start there.

For shaping new initiatives, use this chapter during your planning phase, not after you've already committed to a path. The questions here should influence your design decisions, not just evaluate them after the fact. Think of it as preventive medicine rather than emergency surgery. When you're scoping that new chatbot or predictive model, ask yourself, Have we thought through the collaboration model? Are we clear on our approach to communication? What creative constraints are we building in? These aren't add-ons—they're foundational choices.

Leadership alignment is perhaps where this toolkit shines brightest. In my experience, executives often nod along to the concept of "human-centered AI" without fully agreeing on what it means. This chapter gives you a common vocabulary and concrete discussion points. Use it in strategy sessions, leadership offsites, or even one-on-ones with key stakeholders—the questions force specificity where vagueness usually lives. And specificity, as we know, is where real commitment begins.

The format is flexible by design. You can run this as a workshop with sticky notes and whiteboards, as a survey distributed across teams, or even as a series of focused conversations over coffee. What matters isn't the format—it's the honesty of the assessment and the commitment to act on what you find because a checklist without follow-through is just expensive paper.

Self-assessment checklist

Here's where we get specific. What follows is a comprehensive list of questions, carefully organized under each of the 5Cs we've explored throughout this book. These aren't random conversation starters—each question maps directly back to a call to action from the previous chapters. Think of it as a way to check whether you did what we talked about, or whether it stayed in the realm of good intentions.

The beauty of this approach is that it creates accountability. Every sub-chapter in this book ended with something concrete you could do. Now we're asking: did you? And if not, what's holding you back? Sometimes the answer reveals more about your organization's readiness than any maturity model ever could.

Competence

- Have you mapped AI literacy requirements to specific roles and functions in your organization, moving beyond generic "AI for everyone" training?

- Is your organization investing equally in business acumen for AI professionals and AI literacy for business professionals?

- Have you created structured opportunities for people to practice AI skills in a safe environment before applying them to real work?

- Do you have an AI Academy or similar learning ecosystem that combines modular learning, group environments, and gamification?

- Are leadership skills being evaluated separately from technical expertise when promoting people into AI leadership roles?

- Have you established mechanisms to identify and address both overconfidence (Dunning-Kruger) and underconfidence (Imposter Syndrome) in AI work?

- Does your organization explicitly recognize and develop different "hats" people wear in AI work (therapist, negotiator, detective, etc.)?

- Have you designed clear learning paths that embed AI fluency into everyday work rather than treating it as separate training?

- Is gamification being used both to teach humans about AI and to help AI systems learn more effectively?

- Are you actively preparing your workforce for evolving AI roles and creating pathways for career transitions?

Collaboration

- Have you moved from transactional coordination to true co-creation in your AI projects, with shared ownership and commitment?

- Is your AI governance federated in a way that balances autonomy with alignment, avoiding both chaos and bottlenecks?

- Have you explicitly defined what kind of collaboration model exists between humans and AI in different contexts (co-worker, co-teacher, coach)?

- Are all AI initiatives cross-functional by default, with domain experts involved from day one rather than consulted at the end?

- Have you established MLOps practices that serve as a bridge between strategy and execution, making AI work traceable and reliable?

- Are you following the pain—starting with real problems that frustrate real people rather than impressive but irrelevant showcases?

- Have you legitimized and supported communities of practice that survive organizational changes and foster peer learning?

- For data-hungry AI projects, have you built collaborative labeling processes that treat data curation as strategic work?

- Is trust being actively measured and managed across all your human-AI collaborations, not just assumed?

Communication
- Have you clearly articulated your AI purpose at the intersection of what excites you, aligns with strategy, is ethical, and is feasible?

- Are you framing AI's value differently for different audiences, connecting organizational benefits to personal rewards?

- Have you mapped your stakeholders into personas (visionaries, pragmatists, skeptics, guardians) and tailored your communication accordingly?

- Are you making the invisible work behind AI visible, showing the effort and judgment that goes into making systems work?

- Have you invested in a semantic layer that gives AI the business context it needs to be genuinely useful?

- Are transparency touchpoints built into user experiences, making AI's behavior understandable to non-technical users?

- Have you established clear guidelines for AI conversations, including tone, escalation paths, and human handoffs?

- Are you maintaining flexible voice guidelines that preserve authenticity while ensuring consistency?

Creativity

- Do you have a clear framework for when humans should disrupt and when AI should refine, mapped to different creative tasks?

- Have you shifted focus upstream to ideation and meaning-making as AI accelerates downstream execution?

- Is prompt engineering being treated as a creative discipline with shared libraries and collaborative development?

- Have you defined clear criteria for when to co-create with AI and when human creativity should stand alone?

- Are you actively monitoring and countering the "sameness trap" through diversity audits and originality checks?

- For traditional AI systems, are you recognizing and fostering the creativity in problem formulation and pattern discovery?

- Have you created a culture that makes room to tinker, with psychological safety and dedicated experimentation time?

- Are you participating in open coopetition, contributing to shared tools while differentiating at the edge?

Conscience

- Do you have structured processes for learning from AI failures, both your own and others', using divergent and convergent thinking?

- Have you translated abstract AI principles into concrete practices, checklists, and decision guides?

- Is accountability clearly mapped across model, data, and interface layers with defined ownership and escalation paths?

- Are you maintaining human oversight for moral judgments while designing clear feedback loops between AI and human values?

- Do you have tools and processes in place for detecting and mitigating bias, including diverse perspectives in the review process?

- Have you built verification workflows and transparency markers to combat disinformation at scale?

- Are you tracking and optimizing the environmental impact of your AI initiatives, not just their business impact?

- Have you expanded your success metrics beyond ROI to include Return on Ethics, Trust Retention, and Psychological Safety?

- Is AI ethics truly cross-functional in your organization, showing up in sprint planning rather than compliance reviews?

- Are you clear about what legacy AI systems pose ongoing risks and have plans to address them?

- Have you explicitly discussed and decided which decisions must remain human, regardless of AI capability?

Take your time with these questions. Some will be easy to answer—a clear yes or no. Others might make you pause and think, "Well, sort of, but not really." That's valuable data. The gaps you identify here aren't failures—they're opportunities. And in the next section, we'll talk about what to do with them.

What to do with what you find

So you've answered all the questions and now you're looking at a mix of confident check marks, uncomfortable blanks, and a whole lot of "sort of" answers. First thing: breathe. No organization gets everything right, and perfection isn't the goal. What matters is being honest about where you are right now, because that's the only way to figure out where to go next. The biggest mistake I see teams make here is trying to fix everything at once. That's like trying to remodel your whole house while you're still living in it— sure, you could do it, but why put yourself through that? Instead, look for the gaps that hurt real people the most. Maybe your bias detection is weak, and customers are losing trust. Or perhaps your collaboration is so disorganized that teams are duplicating work, and everyone is exhausted. Start where it hurts most and where fixing it would make the biggest difference.

> *The key to making progress stick is having clear*
> *ownership and realistic timelines.*

Vague commitments to "improve AI transparency" inevitably fade into the background noise of daily work. But when Tinker (that's a callback) from the UX team owns "implementing confidence indicators in our chatbot interface by Q2," things happen. Set quarterly check-ins to revisit these assessments—not because you love meetings, but because AI moves fast and your blind spots shift. What seems fine today might be problematic in three months. What feels impossible now might have an obvious solution by then. This isn't a one-time health check; it's an ongoing practice of organizational self-awareness—one way to do that is through the **Reflect-Act-Reinforce Framework**, described as follows:

- **Reflect**: Gather diverse perspectives on assessment results, identify root causes (not just symptoms), and prioritize based on human impact and feasibility.

- **Act**: Assign specific owners with clear mandates, set concrete milestones with realistic timelines, and start with visible quick wins to build momentum.

- **Reinforce**: Embed improvements into policies and workflows, celebrate progress publicly to maintain energy, and schedule regular reassessments to catch deviations.

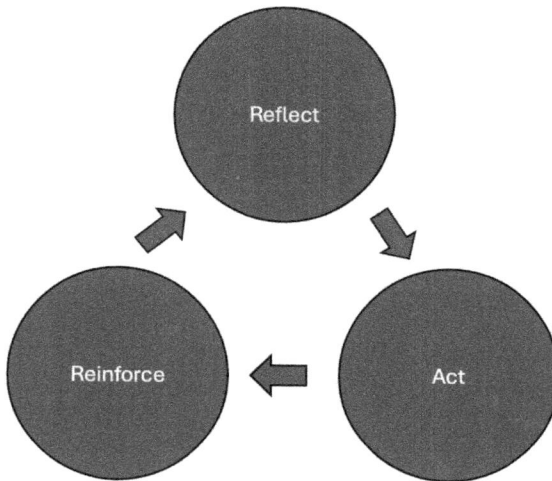

Figure 11: Reflect-Act-Reinforce Cycle.

Living the strategy by making human-centric AI real

A strategy document that sits in a drawer might as well not exist. I've seen too many organizations craft beautiful AI principles, conduct thoughtful assessments, and create detailed action plans, only to watch them all evaporate the moment things get busy. The truth is, a strategy only becomes real when it changes how people work. Not how they say they work in presentations, but what they do when no one's watching. That's why this final section isn't about more planning. It's about embedding these human-centered values so deeply into your organization's DNA that they become as natural as your morning coffee routine.

Start with the small stuff that scales. Update your prompt templates to include ethical considerations by default. Build empathy checks into your model review process. Add "human impact" as a standing agenda item in your AI project meetings. These might seem like tiny changes, but they compound. When every prompt an employee writes naturally considers tone and bias, when every model review automatically includes diverse perspectives, when every project discussion surfaces human implications—that's when strategy becomes culture. And culture, as we know, eats strategy for breakfast.[40]

Now, if you're reading this from a small or medium enterprise (SME), you might be thinking, "This all sounds great, but we're five people and a dog, not Google." Fair point. The good news is that being smaller can be your advantage here. You don't need elaborate governance structures or cross-functional committees when you can shout across the room to your colleague. Select the elements that align with your most significant risks and opportunities. Maybe you're a healthcare startup—then bias detection and accountability matter more than creative voice guidelines. Perhaps you're a local retailer experimenting with AI customer service; then focus on transparency and trust metrics over complex MLOps infrastructure.

The beauty of being smaller is that you can move faster and change course more easily. You don't need six months of change management to update how you work—you can start tomorrow.

---

[40] This quote is attributed most often to management consultant Peter Drucker.

Pick one or two of the 5Cs that resonate most with your current challenges. If you're struggling with AI adoption, start with competence. If you're concerned about customer trust, prioritize clear communication and a genuine conscience. You can always add more as you grow. Remember, even tech giants started in garages—they didn't implement everything on day one either. The key is to start somewhere and build the muscle memory of human-centered thinking into whatever scale you're operating on.

But none of this works without leadership modeling. If your executives discuss human-centered AI but prioritize purely technical metrics, everyone notices. If they preach psychological safety but punish failed experiments, the message is clear. Leaders need to be caught actively using the assessment tools, publicly sharing their own learning struggles with AI, and making decisions that prioritize long-term human value over short-term efficiency gains. They need to ask different questions in reviews—not just "How accurate is the model?" but "How does this affect the people who use it?" Not just "What's the ROI?" but "What's the impact on trust?"

The final piece is recognizing that this is a marathon, not a sprint. AI transformation is inevitable—the question is whether people and culture transformation will keep pace. Every new model deployed, every process automated, every decision augmented is an opportunity to reinforce or erode your human-centered approach. Make the choice conscious. Build strong habits. Because in five years, the organizations that thrive won't be the ones with the most advanced AI. They'll be the ones where AI and humanity learned to dance together, each making the other better. And that dance starts with the next decision you make, the following prompt you write, the next team you gather. The checklist is complete. The real work begins now.

NINE

Conclusion

We've reached the end of this particular journey, but in many ways, we're just at the beginning. Throughout this book, we've explored how to make AI strategy more human through competence, collaboration, communication, creativity, and conscience. We've examined frameworks and tools, shared stories of failures and successes, and hopefully challenged some assumptions about what an AI strategy entails. But here's the thing: none of it matters unless someone—maybe you—decides to lead differently. Because AI's next chapter isn't about who has the most powerful models or the biggest compute budget. It's about who has the wisdom to steward this technology toward outcomes that serve humanity.

The technical capabilities will continue to advance, whether or not we contribute to their development. Models will get larger, faster, and more capable. Costs will drop. Access will spread. That trajectory feels almost inevitable now. What isn't inevitable is how we choose to integrate these capabilities into our organizations, our societies, and our lives. That's where leadership comes in—not the kind that optimizes metrics or hits quarterly targets, but the kind that asks harder questions. The kind that sometimes says *no* when everyone else is saying *yes*. The kind that remembers that behind every data point is a person, and behind every efficiency gain is a human consequence.

Let me paint a picture of what's likely coming, because leading through uncertainty requires at least some sense of what futures we might need to navigate:

- **Multi-agent coordination**: We're moving rapidly toward a world where AI agents don't just assist individual users but coordinate with each other to accomplish complex tasks. Imagine your AI assistant negotiating with a vendor's AI, which checks with its supply chain AI, which coordinates with logistics AIs—all in seconds. The efficiency gains could be staggering, but so could the loss of human oversight and the concentration of power in the hands of those who control the coordination protocols.

- **Broad-capability AGI**: Whether it arrives in five years or 50, artificial general intelligence—systems that match or exceed human cognitive abilities across all domains—could fundamentally reshape every assumption we have about work, creativity, and human purpose. This is no longer science fiction—it's a scenario that serious researchers and organizations are actively preparing for. The question isn't whether we'll need to adapt, but whether we'll have built the ethical frameworks and human safeguards in time.

- **The singularity (self-improving AI systems)**: Perhaps the most profound shift would be AI systems capable of improving themselves without human intervention— each generation designing a better version of itself in an accelerating cycle. While this might sound like pure speculation, the basic ingredients already exist in current research. The implications range from unprecedented scientific breakthroughs to existential risks that make today's AI concerns look quaint.

Nick Bostrom highlighted some of these risks in Superintelligence (Oxford University Press, 2014), particularly in relation to job displacement and rising inequality. While I don't share all of his conclusions—I'm more optimistic about human adaptability than he sometimes appears to be—the core warning is worth considering. The choices we make now regarding AI governance, human agency, and value alignment will have lasting implications for generations to come. We're not just building tools; we're shaping the conditions for whatever comes next.

This brings us to the reflective questions that every leader should be wrestling with. First, what values will remain stable in an unstable future? When everything else is shifting—business models, job definitions, even the nature of intelligence itself—

what north stars can we rely on? For me, it always comes back to human dignity, the importance of meaningful choice, and the irreplaceable value of genuine connection. Your list might be different, but you need to have one.

In the turbulence ahead, these stable values become the anchors that keep us grounded.

Second, which decisions must stay human, no matter how advanced AI becomes? I'm not talking about regulatory requirements or technical limitations. I'm referring to the choices that shape who we are as a species. The decision to bring a new life into the world. The choice to end or extend care for someone we love. The judgment of guilt or innocence when freedom is at stake. The spark of inspiration that creates something genuinely new. These aren't just tasks to be optimized—they're expressions of humanity itself.

The most important thing I can leave you with is this: the future of AI isn't predetermined. It's not locked in some Silicon Valley lab or government planning document. It's being written right now, in millions of small decisions across thousands of organizations. Every time you choose transparency over convenience, every time you prioritize human judgment over pure efficiency, every time you ask "should we?" instead of just "can we?"—you're shaping that future. Every prompt you write, every model you deploy, every team you build is a vote for the kind of world we're creating.

So, yes, understand the technology. Yes, build the strategies. Yes, use the frameworks and run the assessments. But more than any of that, lead with conscience. Lead with creativity. Lead with the unshakeable belief that humans aren't just another variable to be optimized, but the whole reason we're building any of this in the first place. The machines are becoming increasingly intelligent every day. The question is, Are we getting wiser?

The future of AI lies in all of our (human) hands.
Good luck.

About the Author

Tiankai Feng is a Data & AI leader by day, a musician by night, and an optimist at heart. His experiences span marketing analytics, business performance management, data product ownership, capability leadership, data governance, data strategy, and AI transformation. Working at TD Reply, adidas, and Thoughtworks allowed him to experience data and AI challenges from both consultant and client perspectives, helping him identify patterns in what works and what spectacularly doesn't. Author of "Humanizing Data Strategy," TEDx speaker, and frequent keynote presenter, Tiankai strongly believes in keeping humans at the center of our AI future. He often uses humor, music, and perfectly timed memes to make AI less intimidating and more approachable—because if we're going to work with machines that sound human, we might as well have some fun with it.

Index